# RENAL WARRIOR

## DIET COOKBOOK 2022

## 1500 DAYS OF RENAL WARRIOR DIET TO SEND YOUR KIDNEY DISEASE TO HELL WITH THE MOST LOVED RECIPES FROM THE FAN CLUB KITCHEN COMMUNITY

THE
FAN CLUB KITCHEN
KNOWLEDGE COMES FROM A GROUP OF PEOPLE
WITH A DIFFERENT IDEAS
BE THE AUTHOR
WRITTEN BY THE PEOPLE

# Table of Contents

## SOUPS AND STEWS..............................46

## VEGETARIAN RECIPES AND VEGANS....80

## PUB RECIPES....88

## WHOLE FAMILY RECIPES.................................118

# ABOUT FUN CLUB KITCHEN

The Fun Club Kitchen is a community of crazy, innovative people and visionaries who seek to change the culinary world with their collection of knowledge, gleaned from different cultures, traditions, expertise, and experiences.

For years, we have been inundated with cookbooks and diet books written by gurus, experts, and famous chefs, but the naked truth is that 90% of ordinary people will never put them into practice.

The Fun Club Kitchen turns the tables and creates books that are shaped by the readers themselves, going from simple readers to co-authors and contributors. This increases the chances of creating only the most effective books, targeted and tailored to different types of consumers.

But that's not all.

The Fun Club Kitchen gives readers the opportunity to sign with their own name for every single recipe, case study, or improvement of any kind shared with the community, making the most deserving co-authors famous. With the supervision of specialists in every field, The Fun Club Kitchen's arsenal of cookbooks is a strategic mix of value, timeliness, and innovation.

With The Fun Club Kitchen, you will:


- Discover personal notes from people like you.

- Share your unique personalized recipes with thousands of readers.

- Get solutions to problems that only an alliance of expert minds can solve.

- Discover the editions updated year after year, month after month.

To become a member of this crazy revolution, you just need to buy any copy — the rest is up to you!


**Don't just be a reader...Be The Author.... by joining "The Fun Club Kitchen...with its "Written By The People" cookbooks.**

# INTRODUCTION

What you eat and the lifestyle choices you make are very important. If you are diagnosed in the early stages of the disease, there are many steps you can take to prolong your kidney function. When you make positive changes, have patience, and commit to working closely with your healthcare team, there is a good chance that you will be able to enjoy a high-quality, happy and active life.

## WHAT IS KIDNEY DISEASE?

Let's begin by understanding how the kidneys function. Your body has two kidneys that are bean-shaped and about the size of your fist. When the kidneys are working properly, they help keep your whole body in balance by performing the following important tasks:

1. Clean waste materials from your blood.
2. Remove excess water from your body.
3. Regulate your blood pressure.
4. Stimulate your bone marrow to make red blood cells.
5. Control the amount of calcium and phosphorus absorbed and excreted.

When you have chronic kidney disease, your kidneys do not work properly and cannot perform these tasks. Although there is no cure for kidney failure, it is possible to live a long and healthy life with proper treatment and good dietary and lifestyle choices.

## CAUSES

Kidney disease is most often caused by poorly controlled diabetes or high blood pressure. Physical injury and drug toxicity can also damage your kidneys. Kidney disease affects people of all ages and races, but Hispanics, African Americans, and Native Americans tend to have a greater risk of kidney failure. This is mostly due to a higher incidence of diabetes and high blood pressure in these populations.

Uncontrolled diabetes is the primary cause of kidney failure. In fact, 44% of people who start dialysis have kidney failure because of diabetes. Diabetes develops when blood glucose (blood sugar) levels are too high in the body. When our bodies digest protein from the food we eat, the process of digestion creates waste products. In the kidneys, millions of small blood vessels, called capillaries, act as filters. As blood flows through the capillaries, the waste products are filtered out into our urine. Substances such as protein and red blood cells are too big to pass through the capillaries and stay in the blood.

Diabetes damages this process. Too much blood is filtered when there is a high level of blood sugar. All the extra work wears down the filters, and after many years, the filters start to leak. The good protein our bodies need is then filtered out and lost through the urine. Eventually, the kidneys cannot remove the extra waste from the blood. This ultimately leads to kidney damage or failure. This damage can happen over many years without any signs or symptoms. That is why it is so important for people with diabetes to manage their blood-sugar levels and get tested for kidney disease periodically.

High blood pressure is another contributor to kidney disease. One in three Americans with high blood pressure, also known as hypertension, is at risk for kidney disease. High blood pressure is the second leading cause of kidney disease and increases your risk of developing a heart attack or stroke. Treatment and lifestyle changes, including blood-pressure medications, following a healthy diet, and exercising can lower blood pressure.

High blood pressure means the heart has to work harder at pumping blood. As time passes, high blood pressure can harm blood vessels in your body, including the ones in your kidneys—which causes them to stop filtering out waste and extra fluid from your body. The extra fluid in your blood vessels can also make your blood pressure rise, creating a vicious and detrimental cycle. As in diabetes, this damage can happen over many years without any signs or symptoms. It is very important for people with high blood pressure to control their blood pressure and get tested for kidney disease, just like people who have diabetes. High blood pressure is the cause of more than 25,000 new cases of kidney failure in the United States every year.

## SYMPTOMS

Kidney failure is a progressive disease; it does not happen overnight. Some people in the early stages of kidney disease do not show any symptoms. Symptoms usually appear in the upcoming stages of kidney disease.

When the kidneys are damaged, wastes and toxins can build up in your body. Once the buildup starts to occur, you may feel sick and experience some of the following symptoms:

- Nausea
- Weakness
- Poor appetite
- Trouble sleeping
- Itching
- Tiredness
- Weight loss
- Swelling of your feet and ankles
- Muscle cramps (especially in the legs)
- Anemia (low red blood cell count)

The good news is that once you begin treatment for kidney disease, your symptoms and general health will start to improve!

### STAGES OF CHRONIC KIDNEY DISEASE (CKD)

There are five stages of CKD. Each level has a corresponding GFR index that accompanies it. It is very important for someone who has CKD to have continual monitoring of their GFR index because it doesn't take much for the change in the index to trigger the following stage of chronic kidney disease. For this reason alone, it is important to monitor what you are eating in conjunction with your stage of the disease.

## STAGE 1 AND 2 CKD (NORMAL TO HIGH AND MILD GFR)

Most people who have stage one or two chronic kidney disease do not know that they have it. Their GFR index is generally greater than ninety milliliters per minute for stage one, and an index that is sixty to eighty-nine milliliters per minute for stage two. Generally, the people who have been diagnosed with stage one or two CKD were diagnosed because of tests for another illness. Symptoms of stage one and two can be extremely vague, but a good indicator is higher than normal creatinine levels in the blood or urine. With stage two, the filtration levels of the kidney have begun to decrease, but not at an overly noticeable level. People living with stage one and two CKD can still live a normal life, they can't cure their kidneys, but they can help stop or slow the progression of the disease. Keeping blood pressure in line and eating a diet that is renal friendly are good first steps. Your doctor will keep up on your creatine levels and GFR to monitor the progression of CKD.

## STAGE 3A AND 3B (MODERATE GFR)

Stage three is broken up into two GFR indexes, but the symptoms aren't much different. The GFR index for stage A is an index of forty-five to fifty-nine milliliters per minute. The GFR for stage B is thirty to forty-four milliliters per minute. As the kidney's functions decrease, the build-up of wastes causes the body to go into uremia, which is a buildup of that waste in the blood. More complications from kidney failure become apparent. The chances for high blood pressure increase, and patients are likely to exhibit anemia. Swelling, or edema, may start to become apparent because of the water retention and typically starts in the arms and legs. Diet becomes increasingly more important with stage three CDK due to the buildup in the body.

## STAGE 4 (SEVERE GFR)

Stage four is the last stop before kidney failure. The GFR index for stage four is fifteen to twenty-nine milliliters per minute. Stage four patients are more than likely receiving dialysis and are thinking about transplant in the near future. The body is barely filtering the wastes, hence the need for mechanical intervention for filtration. At this stage, edema worsens, and physical symptoms can be overwhelming. Diet in this phase is stricter and will consist of limiting things that can build up in the body which the kidneys are no longer able to take care of on their own.

## STAGE 5 (END STAGE GFR)

Once the kidneys are no longer filtering the waste in the body, dialysis will be necessary to live. The GFR index in the end-stage is less than fifteen milliliters per minute. There is also a chance that if you meet the qualifications, you will be put on a transplant list. Stage five CKD leaves the patient feeling sick almost all of the time because of the toxins and waste built up in the body. A nephrologist, a doctor who specializes in treating kidneys, will be a permanent part of your medical regimen. Diet will be an absolute must, as well as limiting fluid intake.

## HOW TO NATURALLY PREVENT THE NEED FOR DIALYSIS

Dialysis steps in as a last case scenario when both kidneys lose sufficient function to clean the blood. Before the toxicity reaches a damaging level, it must be eradicated through external sources. Individuals who suffer from acute kidney diseases end up going through dialysis to get their blood cleaned through the artificial dialysis machine. This dialysis machine mimics the role of our kidneys, and the blood is pumped into the machine, and then it is pumped back into the body simultaneously.

Those who never went through dialysis should know that it is one long and exhaustive process that every renal patient hates to go through. Fortunately, there are some effective measures to avoid dialysis. This precautionary measure can stop the progression of renal disease and even cure it to some extent.

- Exercise regularly
- Avoid excess salt in your diet
- Don't smoke
- Control of diabetes
- Control high blood pressure
- Eat correctly and lose excess weight
- Talk with your health care team

# CHAPTER 1
## WINNING HABITS THAT PEOPLE WHO MANAGE TO BLOCK THE DISEASE

You would vow to stick to a fitness routine at least once every year. However, if you have had some difficulties with the follow-through, you are definitely in good company. Yet, there are so many motives for making the commitment and continuing with it again.

Everybody's got a different excuse to lose momentum. The bottom line is that it's never too late to start a workout routine if staying healthy is essential to you. And it takes less time than to navigate down the Facebook page; one may fit in a day's work out.

Possibly, when you watch TV, you should do it if you follow organizations such as the ACE (American Council on Exercise) and CDC (Centers for Disease Control & Prevention).

A total of 150 minutes of exercise per week is what you need to boost your cardiac well-being and decrease your chance of all forms of other diseases. It is totally up to you when and how you fit these minutes into your daily routine.

But start now, and use these ideas to help make your workout part of the exercise.

## SET A SMART GOAL

A SMART purpose, according to ACE, is to be:

- Specific
- Measurable measurements
- Achievable
- Right
- Time

## PERIOD (FULFILLED WITH A DEADLINE AND COMPLETED IN A SPECIFIED PERIOD)

Having objectives helps to offer concentration and order to what you wish to do. Meeting targets is rewarding because it helps create excitement, exercise experts claim. Only pay particular attention to the portion of this equation that is "attainable."

Just an impossible target sets you up to struggle. Instead of forcing yourself to exercise every day for 30 minutes of the week because you can't even squeeze in 15 on other days, look at your calendar to find two days when you can raise your gym period to 30 minutes reasonably. All adds up to get you to your 150-minute week target.

## VOWING TO TAKE MORE STEPS EACH DAY

For almost a decade, public health specialists at the CDC have encouraged Americans to take 10,000 steps per day. The 10,000 level averages out at around 5 miles a day, and "healthy" are known to be those that exercise as far. Those that get in 12,500 steps a day are "very involved." Even if weight reduction is not your priority, you can improve your everyday mileage to attain or sustain overall healthy health.

## RENDER EXERCISE A WAY OF LIFE, NOT A FAD

Some individuals make the error of going hard for exercise targets, but they slacken off after being reached. They use fitness as a means to a goal, not a way of living their lives. This will result in health conditions and weight gain. Failure to see health as a lifestyle option ensures that daily activity's long-term advantages would not be reaped.

Sure, in the short term, exercising will help you reduce or retain weight. Yet lifelong gains are created by an active lifestyle. It will lower the risk of future health problems, including:

- Elevated Blood Pressure
- Diabetes Nausea
- Cardiac Disorder
- Obesity

Exercise leads to better well-being and wellness, so make it a priority-it's never too late.

## FOR KIDNEY FAILURE, WHAT FOODS DO YOU EAT?

This may be a little complicated at first to put together a good renal disease meal program, particularly if you don't know which foods you shouldn't eat with renal disease. People also want to think too deeply about what they cannot feed that they get overwhelmed to the extent that they don't know how much you can consume on a renal diet versus what you can eat. The trick is to reflect on the key Ingredients you can avoid while still reflecting on the several choices that you do have available.

Here are a few explanations of kidney disorder foods that you can eat:

## FOODS UNPROCESSED

In the U.S., in particular, people appear to rely on packaged foods to make their meals. Such goods are full of additives that are not safe for anybody, including an individual with renal disease. Huge quantities of salt and lots of other additives are loaded with packaged foods like canned cheese and macaroni meal helper sets and even plain rice dishes, which come in a package. As a common concept, you shouldn't consume anything if it arrives in a wooden box. You should instead depend on the natural foods that can help the body regenerate and fill you up. When you're about to make any changes, learning what you should consume on a kidney diet helps. Without the additional preservatives, discover methods to make your preferred dishes from scratch.

## THE NATURAL PRODUCE

Sometimes, vegetables and fruit are considered natural medications for your health, so the produce department is always a perfect way to start while you search for groceries. It should always be in your cart or on your dining table, especially foods like bell peppers, onions, cabbage, and super-foods such as berries. Ensure that you're still paying care to your potassium consumption if you're in the latter stages of kidney disease, which may reduce your development choices a little more. You may ask what foods are produced not to consume with renal disease, but this depends on your process and diet limits. Check for more choices with our meal preparation solution: 21 Day Pre-Dialysis Kidney Disease Vegetarian Meal Schedule

## THE APPROPRIATE GRAINS

Although your kidneys might not have processed some whole grain choices, you may always appreciate stuff like pasta and rice in moderation. To make it simpler for the kidneys to absorb your consuming meal byproducts due to potassium & phosphorus limits, sticking to these ingredients' white varieties. You will appreciate the whole grain forms to raise fiber if you are not limited (Stage 3 / 4 CKD).

## SPICES AND HERBS

To make meals taste nice, you do not need salt. If you sprinkle in numerous spices, which is part of foods you may eat on a renal diet, you may begin to find that foods naturally taste more delightful and have deeper flavors than you have ever thought possible. Go for new or dried herbs & spices (salt-free) to season your meals anytime you need anything special to dress up the recipes.

## LEAN PROTEINS

You might be or might not need to restrict the protein consumption, based on what process of renal disease you're in. However, it is recommended that most patients also have a serving of lean protein at least once a day. Normally, fish, egg whites, poultry, and tofu are the top options. Fish is particularly good for you, as it gives your diet with good healthy omega 3s. To create great and satisfying meals, you can use any of these options, and the choices are only as restricted as your imagination. Consider tacos, fajitas, casseroles, and much more, beginning with these excellent lean protein options.

You will start to create a tasty and balanced renal disease meal schedule, beginning with any of these food groups & examples. Before creating a new diet, decisions or changing drastically what you consume for your renal illness, always consult a doctor.

# CHAPTER 2
## DIET

## CONTROL YOUR DIET WITH KIDNEY DISEASE

When you have chronic kidney disease, controlling what you eat and drink can be a challenge; however, your diet can also positively influence how you feel and what other treatments you may need.

An experienced dietitian certified kidney disease expert. The best person to ask for a personalized meal plan is a kidney dietitian. A dietary assessment to determine the energy consumption and important nutrients will be the first step.

Dietary assessment includes a review of energy consumption and important nutrients such as:

- Sodium salts
- Potassium
- Phosphate
- Liquids
- Fat

Dietary advice is given personally, based on what you like to eat, how you feel, your age, your lifestyle, your weight, your muscle size, your health status and your test results.

Everyone should limit the consumption of salt, sugar and fat as part of a healthy lifestyle.

With the time of kidney disease, your dietary needs are likely to change. Your kidneys will be less effective in eliminating unwanted fluids and controlling the correct levels of nutrients such as calcium, phosphate and potassium.

The recommended initial dietary change may be small, but as your kidney disease progresses, further changes may be needed.

### HOW TO MAKE THE MOST OF YOUR KIDNEY DIETITIAN APPOINTMENT

A few days before the appointment, write down what you eat and bring the list.

Take a list of your medications.

If someone else is cooking for you, ask them to accompany you.

Ask questions to trust what you need to do and why.

Regularly schedule follow-up appointments to track your progress.

## MAINTAIN A HEALTHY WEIGHT

Malnutrition can develop when food intake is insufficient, and your body does not get the right amount of vitamins, minerals and other nutrients. This is most common in the later stages of chronic kidney failure.

If you lose weight that you weren't expecting or are worried about your diet, tell your doctor or kidney nutritionist.

Weight gain can also cause serious health problems. If you are overweight, dialysis may be more difficult to access and may not be suitable for a kidney transplant. If weight gain is a problem, your kidney nutritionist can help you plan a proper diet plan.

Before taking dietary supplements or starting a plan to lose or increase weight loss, always consult your doctor or kidney nutritionist. Changes in food and water are potentially serious and cause significant harm.

## TIPS ON VITAMINS AND MINERALS

If you do not get all the vitamins and minerals you need from the foods you eat, your doctor or dietitian may recommend or prescribe vitamins and minerals supplements, depending on the stage of your kidney disease.

Usually, a well-balanced diet will provide you with enough vitamins and minerals to keep you healthy. However, dialysis treatment will eliminate certain water-soluble vitamins from the body.

When you are on dialysis, you should take only vitamin supplements that are recommended because some vitamins and minerals can be harmful. It is important that you consult your doctor.

Vitamins can be helpful in supplementing your health when you have or experience any of the following symptoms:

- Chronically or irregular eating habits
- Decreased appetite, nausea, vomiting
- Changes in taste or aversion to food
- Unwanted weight loss
- Food insecurity
- Vitamin loss during dialysis.

# CHAPTER 3
## PHYSICAL EXERCISE

One of the most important ways to keep fit and healthy is by staying active and engaging in regular exercise. Regular movement is key, and exercise is different for everyone, depending on their abilities and options available. Fortunately, there are unlimited ways to customize an exercise routine or plan that can suit any lifestyle, perhaps low impact to start, or if you're ready, engage in a more vigorous workout. For many people experiencing kidney disease, one of the major struggles is losing weight and living a sedentary life, where movement is generally minimal and exercise is not generally practiced. Smoking, eating processed foods, and not getting the required nutrition can further impair the body in such a way that exercise is seen as a hurdle and a challenge that is best avoided. Making lifestyle changes is not something that should be done all at once, but over a period of time—especially during the early stages of renal disease—so that the impact of the condition is minimized over time and becomes more manageable.

Where can you begin, if you haven't exercised at all or for a long period of time? For starters, don't sign up for a marathon or engage in any strenuous activities unless it is safe to do so. Start slow, and take your time. Before taking on any new movements – whether it is minimal, low-impact walking or stretching, or a more moderate to the high-impact regimen—always talk to your doctor to rule out any impact this may have on other existing conditions, such as blood pressure and respiratory conditions, as well as your kidneys. Most, if not all, physicians will likely recommend exercise as part of the treatment plan, but may advise beginning slowly if your body isn't used to exercise.

Simple techniques to introduce exercise into your life require a commitment. This can begin with a quick 15-minute walk or jog and a 10- or 15-minute stretch in the morning before starting your day. There are a number of easy, introductory techniques to consider, including the following:

- Take a walk for 10 to 15 minutes each day, at least three or four days each week. If you find it difficult at first, due to cramping, respiratory issues, or other conditions, walk slowly and breathe deeply. Make sure you feel relaxed during your walks. Find a scenic path or area in your neighborhood that is pleasant and gives you something to enjoy, such as a beautiful sunset or forested park. Bring a bottle of water to keep yourself hydrated.

- Stretch for five minutes once a day. This doesn't mean you need to do any intricate yoga poses or specific techniques. In fact, moving your ankles, wrists, and arms in circles and standing every so often (if you sit often) and twisting your torso can help release stress and improve your blood flow, which lowers blood pressure and helps your body transport nutrients to areas in need of repair.

- Practice breathing long, measured breaths. This will help prepare you for more endurance-based exercise, such as jogging, long walks, cycling, and swimming. Count to five on each inhale and exhale, and practice moving slowly as you breathe, to "sync" or coordinate your body's movements with your breathing. If you have difficulty with the respiratory system, take it slow and don't push yourself. If you feel weak or out of breath, stop immediately and try again later or the next day at a slower pace.

- Start a beginner's yoga class and learn the fundamentals of various poses and stretches. It is helpful to arrive early and speak with the instructor, who can provide guidance on which modifications work best if needed. They may also be able to provide tips on how to approach certain poses or movements that can be challenging for beginners so that you feel more comfortable and knowledgeable before you start.

- If you smoke, exercise will present more of a challenge to your lungs and respiratory function. Once you become accustomed to a beginner's level and become moderately active, you may notice it takes more effort, which requires an increase in lung capacity and oxygen. Smoking will eventually present a challenge, and where quitting can be a long-term and difficult goal in itself, make an effort to cut back as much as it takes to allow your body's movements and exercise to continue. In time, you may find quitting becomes easier and more achievable than expected!

- Once you get into a basic routine, there is a wide variety of individual and team activities to consider for your life. If you are a social person, joining a baseball team or badminton club may be ideal. For more solitary options, consider swimming, cycling, or jogging. Many gyms and community centers provide monthly plans and may offer a free trial period to see if their facilities work for you. This is a great opportunity to try new classes and equipment to gauge how much you can achieve, even if in the early stages of exercise so that you can decide whether to pursue dance aerobics, spin classes and/or weight training. Some gyms will provide a free consultation with a personal trainer to set a simple plan towards weight loss and strength training goals.

## THE BENEFITS OF EXERCISE FOR KIDNEY HEALTH

When you begin a new form of exercise, it may not seem like a benefit at first. The aching and stretched muscles and the odd sensation of moving your body more than usual may be unpleasant, though it will gradually become unnoticeably less over time, replaced with a sensation of feeling "worked out" rather than "worn out." Within just a few weeks, you'll notice a significant change in how you feel. Lower blood pressure, reduced stress levels, and even weight loss may be noticeable within just two weeks of moderate, but regular exercise.

# CHAPTER 4
## LEARN TO COOK

Learning to cook your own food is one of the most important things you can do to preserve your health. Cooking is not difficult and does not need to take a lot of time. Provided that you can read, you can learn how to cook, and I am going to tell you how. Of course, if a fair amount of time is inconvenient for you, you can pay someone else to cook for you. I had all sorts of help when I was trying to get back on my feet.

If you are too intimidated to cook, and it would take several more pages just to teach you how to read and cook at the same time, you can be the type of person who eats a lot of fast food instead of making your own healthy food. I hope that I am not alone in considering that no one should be forced to choose fast food when healthy alternatives are far more convenient and healthier.

Cooking for yourself, your family, and anyone else you feed can be a relaxing, enjoyable activity. Cooking can be fun! It is a shame to miss out on that part of life because someone insists that it is difficult.

I want you to know that my situation is atypical. I worked through some really challenging health issues, including some that were initially misdiagnosed. All of my doctors were quickly frustrated with my situation and refused to work with me on all of my symptoms. I was told that I just needed to "deal with it." Needing help does not mean that you are weak, stupid, or doomed to a life of suffering. There are many great resources for people who have special health needs. If your doctors are not open to listening, you can take your vision and passion to a new doctor. My husband took me to three different doctors in one day, and together they found the missing pieces of my puzzle. One of the three was on staff at Mercy Medical Center in Baltimore. He was the only one who was willing to write a prescription for my journey and join me on it.

If you are unhappy with your life and you are worried about your health, you need to keep looking until you find someone who is willing to work with you. You are not going to be abandoned. You will be able to evaluate your worth for yourself. Work with a doctor who is open to working with you. There is someone out there for you. You are not alone.

## TAKE TIME AND LEARN A SKILL

It takes time to learn a skill, but the process itself can be enjoyable. It doesn't need to be a miserable and frustrating experience. My skills improved over time, and I learned many things about cooking that I will never forget. I would never have guessed a few years back that I would someday be writing about healthy cooking. If you are a full-time caregiver, or you are in school, you may not have the time or the energy to cook six or seven times a week. Maybe you will pick up some skills at school to handle the little food preparation you need to do. Work with the situation that you are in and don't give up. Don't let someone convince you that you are so incapable and weak. . . get back on your feet.I was hospitalized many times, but when I was home I would constantly be cooking. If I wasn't cooking, I really didn't feel good. When I cooked, it was a little food after a meal, or a little snack after school, or for no reason at all, if I wasn't good, tired, or didn't feel up to it.In the beginning, I didn't have a recipe book, and I wanted to know how to do things all by myself. I had no time to buy a recipe book, so I would make up my own. I would make food from scratch again and again until something I had made tasted good enough to serve to my family and other friends. Slowly, I started to pick up a few tricks. One day I found a small book of steak recipes on the shelf of my aunt's kitchen. I thought I should learn how to cook steak. It didn't take long for me to realize that I had nothing to learn from that book. There was no substitute for reading cookbooks and using them as a reference. Cooking is an art that is similar to music, painting, writing, and all sorts of other creative and artistic endeavors. I think it is a shame that we cover up our creativity and skills with food.

This renal diet cookbook will give you lots of great new recipes. I am going to teach you how to cook for yourself, your friends, your family, and the people you love. I am going to teach you how to cook kidney-friendly meals and snacks from scratch.

# CHAPTER 5
## FOOD TO EAT AND TO AVOID

Many foods work well within the renal diet. Once you see the available variety, it will not seem as restrictive or difficult to follow. The key is to focus on foods with a high level of nutrients, making it easier for the kidneys to process the waste by not adding too much that the body needs to discard. Balance is a major factor in maintaining and improving long-term renal function.

- **Garlic:** An excellent, vitamin-rich food for the immune system, garlic is a tasty substitute for salt in various dishes. It acts as a significant source of vitamin C and B6, while aiding the kidneys in ridding the body of unwanted toxins. It's a great and healthy way to add flavor to skillet meals, pasta, soups, and stews.

- **Berries:** All berries are considered a good renal diet food due to their high level of fiber, antioxidants, and delicious taste, making them an easy option to include as a light snack or as an ingredient in smoothies, salads, and light desserts. Just one handful of blueberries can provide almost one day's vitamin C requirement, as well as a boost of fiber, which is good for weight loss and maintenance.

- **Bell peppers:** Flavorful and easy to enjoy both raw and cooked; bell peppers offer a good vitamin C source, vitamin A, and fiber. Along with other kidney-friendly foods, they make the detoxification process much easier while boosting your body's nutrient level to prevent further health conditions and reduce existing deficiencies.

- **Onions:** This nutritious and tasty vegetable is excellent as a companion to garlic in many dishes or on its own. Like garlic, onions can provide flavor as an alternative to salt and provide a good source of vitamin C, vitamin B, manganese, and fiber, as well. Adding just one quarter or half of the onion is often enough for most meals because of its strong and spicy flavor.

- **Macadamia nuts:** If you enjoy nuts and seeds as snacks, you may learn that many contain high amounts of phosphorus and should be avoided or limited as much as possible. Fortunately, macadamia nuts are an easier option to digest and process, as they contain much lower amounts of phosphorus and make an excellent substitute for other nuts. They are a good source of other nutrients, such as vitamin B, copper, manganese, iron, and healthy fats.

- **Pineapple:** Unlike other high potassium fruits, pineapple is an option that can be enjoyed more often than bananas and kiwis. Citrus fruits are generally high in potassium as well, so if you find yourself craving an orange or grapefruit, choose pineapple instead. In addition to providing high vitamin B and fiber levels, pineapples can reduce inflammation thanks to an enzyme called bromelain.

- **Mushrooms:** In general, mushrooms are a safe and healthy option for the renal diet, especially the shiitake variety, high in selenium, vitamin B, and manganese. They contain a moderate amount of plant-based protein, which is easier for your body to digest and use than animal proteins. Shiitake and portobello mushrooms are often used in vegan diets as a meat substitute due to their texture and pleasant flavor.

## FOODS TO AVOID

Eating restrictions might be different depending upon your level of kidney disease. If you are in the early stages of kidney disease, you may have different restrictions than those in end-stage renal disease or kidney failure. In contrast to this, people with an end-stage renal disease requiring dialysis will face different eating restrictions. Let's discuss some of the foods to avoid while being on the renal diet.

Dark-Colored Colas contain calories, sugar, phosphorus, etc. They contain phosphorus to enhance flavor, increase its life, and avoid discoloration, which can be found in a product's ingredient list. This addition of phosphorus varies depending on the type of cola. Mostly, the dark-colored colas contain 50–100 mg in a 200-ml serving. Therefore, dark colas should be avoided on a renal diet.

Avocados are a source of many nutritious characteristics, plus their strong fats, fiber, and antioxidants. Individuals suffering from kidney disease should avoid them because they are rich in potassium. 150 grams of an avocado provides a whopping 727 mg of potassium. Therefore, avocados, including guacamole, must be avoided on a renal diet, especially if you are on parole to watch your potassium intake.

Canned foods, including soups, vegetables, and beans, are low in cost but contain high amounts of sodium due to salt and increasing its life. Due to this amount of sodium inclusion in canned goods, it is better for people with kidney disease should avoid consumption. Opt for lower-sodium content with the label "no salt added." One more way is to drain or rinse canned foods, such as canned beans and tuna, which could decrease the sodium content by 33–80%, depending on the product.

Brown rice is a whole grain containing a higher concentration of potassium and phosphorus than its white rice counterpart. One cup already cooked brown rice possesses about 150 mg of phosphorus and 154 mg of potassium. In contrast, one cup already cooked white rice has about 69 mg of phosphorus and 54 mg of potassium. Bulgur, buckwheat, pearled barley, and couscous are equally beneficial, low-phosphorus options and might be a good alternative instead of brown rice.

Bananas are high potassium content, low in sodium, and provides 422 mg of potassium per banana. It might disturb your daily balanced potassium intake to 2,000 mg if a banana is a daily staple.

Whole-Wheat bread may harm individuals with kidney disease. But for healthy individuals, it is recommended over refined, white flour bread. White bread is recommended instead of whole-wheat varieties for individuals with kidney disease because it has phosphorus and potassium. If you add more bran and whole grains to the bread, then the amount of phosphorus and potassium contents increases.

Oranges and orange juice are enriched with vitamin C content and potassium. 184 grams provides 333 mg of potassium and 473 mg of potassium in one cup orange juice. With these calculations, they must be avoided or used in a limited amount while being on a renal diet. Other alternatives for oranges and orange juice are apples, grapes, and cinder or juices as they possess low potassium contents.

Potatoes and sweet potatoes, which are potassium-rich vegetables with 156g, contains 610 mg of potassium, whereas 114 g contains 541 mg of potassium, which is relatively high. Like potatoes and sweet potatoes, some of the high- potassium foods could also be soaked or leached to lessen the concentration of potassium contents. Cut them into small and thin pieces and boil those for at least 10 minutes can reduce the potassium content by about 50%. Potatoes that are soaked in a wide pot of water for as low as four hours before cooking could possess even less potassium content than those not soaked before cooking. This is known as "potassium leaching" or the "double cook Direction."

Snack foods like pretzels, chips, and crackers lack nutrients and are much higher in salt. It is very easy to take above the suggested portion, which leads to even greater salt intake than planned. If chips, being made from potatoes, they will contain a significant amount of potassium as well.

If you are suffering or living with kidney disease, reducing your potassium, phosphorus, and sodium intake is essential for managing and tackling the disease. The foods with high-potassium, high-sodium, and high-phosphorus content listed above should always be limited or avoided. These restrictions and nutrients intakes may differ depending on the level of damage to your kidneys. Following a renal diet might be a daunting procedure and a restrictive one most of the time. Working with your physician and nutrition specialist and a renal dietitian can help you formulate a renal diet specific to your individual needs.

# CHAPTER 6

# CONTROL BLOOD PRESSURE AND DIABETES

One of the most effective therapies in managing kidney disease and diabetes is diet. You will need to work with a dietitian to develop an eating plan that's right for you if you have been diagnosed with kidney disease as a result of diabetes. This strategy will help control the levels of blood glucose and reduce the amount of waste and fluid processed by the kidneys.

## WHICH NUTRIENTS DO I NEED TO REGULATE?

Your dietician will provide you with dietary instructions that tell you how much protein, fat, and carbohydrates you will consume, and how much potassium, sodium, and phosphorus you can consume each day. Since these minerals need to be lower in your diet, you can restrict or eliminate those foods when planning your meals.

Portion control is also important. Speak with your dietitian about tips for measuring a serving size accurately. What can be measured on a regular diet as one serving may count as three servings on the kidney diet.

In order to maintain your blood glucose at an even level, the doctor and dietitian will also recommend that you eat meals and snacks of the same size and carbohydrate/calorie content at certain times of the day. It is vital that blood glucose levels are always tested, and the results are shared with your doctor.

## WHAT CAN I EAT?

An example of food choices that are commonly recommended on a standard renal diabetic diet is given below. This list is focused on the inclusion of foods containing sodium, phosphorus, potassium, and high sugar content. Ask your dietitian if you can have any of the listed foods and ensure you know what the recommended serving size should be.

## CARBOHYDRATE FOODS

### MILK AND NONDAIRY

| RECOMMENDED | AVOID |
| --- | --- |
| Non-dairy creamer, plain yogurt, skim or fat-free milk, sugar-free pudding, sugar-free ice cream, sugar-free yogurt, sugar-free non-dairy frozen desserts* <br><br> *Portions of dairy products are often limited to four ounces due to high potassium, phosphorus or protein content | Oilmilk, sweetened yogurt, chocolate milk, sugar-sweetened, sugar-sweetened ice cream, pudding, sugar-sweetened nondairy frozen desserts |

### BREADS AND STARCHES

| RECOMMENDED | AVOID |
| --- | --- |
| Sourdough, whole grain bread and whole wheat, unsweetened, white, wheat, rye, cream of wheat, grits, malt-o-meal, rice, bagel (small), refined dry cereals, noodles, white or whole wheat pasta, cornbread (made from scratch), flour tortilla, hamburger bun, unsalted crackers | Frosted or sugar-coated cereals, bran bread, gingerbread, pancake mix, cornbread mix, instant cereals, bran or granola, biscuits, salted snacks including: potato chips, corn chips and crackers Whole wheat cereals like oatmeal, wheat flakes and raisin bran, and whole-grain hot cereals contain more potassium and phosphorus than refined products. |

## FRUITS AND JUICES

| RECOMMENDED | AVOID |
| --- | --- |
| Applesauce, apricot halves, apples, apple juice, berries including: cranberries, blackberries and blueberries, strawberries, raspberries, low sugar cranberry juice, grapes, grape juice, kumquats, cherries, fruit cocktail, grapefruit, plums, tangerine, watermelon, mandarin oranges, pears, pineapple, fruit canned in unsweetened juice | Bananas, cantaloupe, avocados, dried fruits including: raisins, dates, and prunes, kumquats, star fruit, fresh pears, honeydew melon, kiwis, mangos, oranges and orange juice, tomatoes, papaya, nectarines, pomegranate, fruit canned in syrup |

## STARCHY VEGETABLES

| RECOMMENDED | AVOID |
| --- | --- |
| Mixed vegetables with corn and peas (eat these less often because they are high in phosphorus), corn, peas, potatoes (soaked to reduce potassium) | Yams, baked beans, baked potatoes, sweet potatoes, dried beans (kidneys, pinto or soy, lima, lentil), succotash, winter squash, pumpkin |

## NON-STARCHY VEGETABLES

| RECOMMENDED | AVOID |
| --- | --- |
| Brussels sprouts, carrots, asparagus, beets, broccoli, cabbage, cauliflower, celery, cucumber, green beans, iceberg lettuce, eggplant, frozen broccoli cuts, kale, leeks, red and green peppers, mustard greens, okra, onions, radishes, raw spinach (1/2 cup), summer squash, turnips, snow peas | Beet greens, cactus, cooked Chinese cabbage, Artichoke, fresh bamboo shoots, kohlrabi, rutabagas, tomatoes, tomato sauce or paste, sauerkraut, cooked spinach, tomato juice, vegetable juice |

## HIGHER-PROTEIN FOODS

## MEATS, CHEESES AND EGGS

| RECOMMENDED | AVOID |
| --- | --- |
| Lean cuts of meat, fish, poultry, and seafood; eggs, low cholesterol egg substitute; cottage cheese (limited due to high sodium content) | Bacon, cheeses, hot dogs, canned and luncheon meats, organ meats, salami, salmon, sausage, nuts, pepperoni |

## HIGHER-FAT FOODS

### SEASONING AND CALORIES

| RECOMMENDED | AVOID |
|---|---|
| Tub or soft margarine low in trans fats, cream cheese, low-fat mayonnaise, mayonnaise, sour cream, low-fat cream cheese, low-fat sour cream | Bacon fat, Crisco®, lard, shortening, back fat, oil, margarine high in trans fats, whipping cream |

### BEVERAGES

| RECOMMENDED | AVOID |
|---|---|
| Water, clear diet sodas, lemonade sweetened or homemade tea with an artificial sweetener | Regular or diet dark colas, fruit-flavored drinks or water sweetened with fruit juices, beer, fruit juices, bottled or lemonade containing sugar or canned iced tea, syrup, or phosphoric acid; tea or lemonade sweetened with real sugar |

You may also be instructed to avoid or limit the following salty and sweet foods:

- Honey
- Molasses
- Baked goods
- Candy
- Canned foods
- Condiments
- Onion, garlic or table salt
- Chocolate Regular sugar

- Syrup
- Ice cream
- TV dinners
- Meat tenderizer
- Salted chips and snacks
- Marinades
- Nuts
- Pizza

# CHAPTER 8
## BREAKFAST

BE PART OF THIS COMMUNITY OF CRAZY INNOVATORS AND SHARE
YOUR UNCONVENTIONAL KNOWLEDGE...BE PART OF ...
FUN CLUB KITCHEN

## 1. VEGETABLE OMELET

**Preparation Time:** 15 minutes
**Cooking Time:** 10 minutes
**Servings:** 3
**Ingredients:**

- Egg whites – 4
- Egg – 1
- Chopped fresh parsley – 2 tablespoons.
- Water – 2 tablespoons.
- Olive oil spray
- Chopped and boiled red bell pepper – ½ cup
- Chopped scallion – ¼ cup, both green and white parts
- Ground black pepper

### Directions:

1. Whisk together the egg, egg whites, parsley, and water until well blended. Set aside.
2. Spray a skillet with olive oil spray and place over medium heat.
3. Sauté the peppers and scallion for 3 minutes or until softened.
4. Over the vegetables, you can now pour the egg and cook, swirling the skillet, for 2 minutes or until the edges start to set. Cook until set.
5. Season with black pepper and serve.

### Nutrition:

Calories: 77 - Fat: 3g Carb: 2g - Phosphorus: 67mg -Potassium: 194mg - Sodium: 229mg - Protein: 12g

## 2. MEXICAN STYLE BURRITOS

**Preparation Time:** 5 minutes
**Cooking Time:** 15 minutes
**Servings:** 2
**Ingredients:**

- Olive oil – 1 tablespoon
- Corn tortillas – 2
- Red onion – ¼ cup, chopped
- Red bell peppers – ¼ cup, chopped
- Red chili – ½, deseeded and chopped
- Eggs – 2
- Juice of 1 lime
- Cilantro – 1 tablespoon chopped

### Directions:

1. Turn the broiler to medium heat and place the tortillas underneath for 1 to 2 minutes on each side or until lightly toasted.
2. Remove and keep the broiler on.
3. Sauté onion, chili and bell peppers for 5 to 6 minutes or until soft.
4. Place the eggs on top of the onions and peppers and place skillet under the broiler for 5-6 minutes or until the eggs are cooked.
5. Serve half the eggs and vegetables on top of each tortilla and sprinkle with cilantro and lime juice to serve.

### Nutrition:

Calories: 202 Fat: 13g Carb: 19g Phosphorus: 184mg Potassium: 233mg Sodium: 77mg Protein: 9g

## 3. SWEET PANCAKES
### by June Marco – Brookfield

**Preparation Time:** 10 minutes
**Cooking Time:** 5 minutes
**Servings:** 5
**Ingredients:**

- All-purpose flour – 1 cup
- Stevia – 2 tablespoons
- Baking powder – 2 teaspoons.
- Egg whites – 2
- Almond milk - 1 cup
- Olive oil - 2 tablespoons.
- Maple extract – 1 tablespoon

### Directions:

1. Combine the flour, stevia and baking powder in a bowl.
2. Make a well in the center and place to one side.
3. Mx the egg whites, milk, oil, and maple extract, do this in another bowl.
4. Add the egg mixture to the well and gently mix until a batter is formed.
5. Heat skillet over medium heat.
6. Cook 2 minutes on each side or until the pancake is golden only add 1/5 of the batter to the pan.
7. Repeat with the remaining batter and serve.

**Nutrition:**
Calories: 178 Potassium: 126mg Sodium: 297mg Protein: 6g

## 4. BREAKFAST SMOOTHIE
by Shirley Anderson – Huntsville

**Preparation Time:** 15 minutes
**Cooking Time:** 0 minute
**Servings:** 2

**Ingredients:**
- Frozen blueberries – 1 cup
- Pineapple chunks – ½ cup
- English cucumber – ½ cup
- Apple – ½
- Water – ½ cup

**Directions:**
1. Put the pineapple, blueberries, cucumber, apple, and water in a blender and blend until thick and smooth.
2. Pour into 2 glasses and serve.

**Nutrition:**
Calories: 87 Fat: G Carb: 22g Phosphorus: 28mg Potassium: 192mg Sodium: 3mg Protein: 0.7g

## 5. BUCKWHEAT AND GRAPEFRUIT PORRIDGE
by Sarah Jones – Wyoming

**Preparation Time:** 5 minutes
**Cooking Time:** 20 minutes
**Servings:** 2

**Ingredients:**
- Buckwheat – ½ cup
- Grapefruit – ¼, chopped
- Honey – 1 tablespoon
- Almond milk – 1 ½ cups
- Water – 2 cups

**Directions:**
1. Boil water on the stove. Add the buckwheat and place the lid on the pan.
2. Simmer for 7 to 10 minutes, in a low heat. Check to ensure water does not dry out.

3. Remove and set aside for 5 minutes, do this when most of the water is absorbed.
4. Drain excess water from the pan and stir in almond milk, heating through for 5 minutes.
5. Add the honey and grapefruit.
6. Serve.

**Nutrition:**
Calories: 231 Fat: 4g Carb: 43g Phosphorus: 165mg Potassium: 370mg Sodium: 135mg

## 6. EGG AND VEGGIE MUFFINS
by Linda Chambless – Kearns

**Preparation Time:** 15 minutes
**Cooking Time:** 20 minutes
**Servings:** 4

**Ingredients:**
- Cooking spray
- Eggs – 4
- Unsweetened rice milk – 2 tablespoons
- Sweet onion – ½, chopped
- Red bell pepper – ½, chopped
- Pinch red pepper flakes
- Pinch ground black pepper

**Directions:**
1. Preheat the oven to 350f.
2. Spray 4 muffin pans with cooking spray. Set aside.
3. Whisk together the milk, eggs, onion, red pepper, parsley, red pepper flakes, and black pepper until mixed.
4. Pour the egg mixture into prepared muffin pans.
5. Bake until the muffins are puffed and golden, about 18 to 20 minutes. Serve

**Nutrition:**
Calories: 84 Fat: 5g Carb: 3g Phosphorus: 110mg Potassium: 117mg Sodium: 75mg Protein: 7g

## 7. CHERRY BERRY BULGUR BOWL
**Preparation Time:** 15 minutes
**Cooking Time:** 15 minutes
**Servings:** 4

## Ingredients:

- 1 cup medium-grind bulgur
- 2 cups water
- Pinch salt
- 1 cup halved and pitted cherries or 1 cup canned cherries, drained
- ½ cup raspberries
- ½ cup blackberries
- 1 tablespoon cherry jam
- 2 cups plain whole-milk yogurt

## Directions:

1. Mix the bulgur, water, and salt in a medium saucepan. Do this in a medium heat. Bring to a boil.
2. Reduce the heat to low and simmer, partially covered, for 12 to 15 minutes or until the bulgur is almost tender. Cover, and let stand for 5 minutes to finish cooking do this after removing the pan from the heat.
3. While the bulgur is cooking, combine the raspberries and blackberries in a medium bowl. Stir the cherry jam into the fruit.
4. When the bulgur is tender, divide among four bowls. Top each bowl with ½ cup of yogurt and an equal amount of the berry mixture and serve.

## Nutrition:

Calories: 242 Total Fat: 6g Saturated Fat: 3g Sodium: 85mg Phosphorus: 237mg Potassium: 438mgCarbohydrates: 44g Fiber: 7g Protein: 9gSugar: 13g

## 8.  SAUSAGE BREAKFAST CASSEROLE

Preparation Time:10 minutes
Cooking Time: 50 minutes
Servings: 8
Ingredients:

- 12 eggs
- 1 lb. ground Italian sausage
- 2 ½ tomatoes, sliced
- 3 tbsp. coconut flour
- ¼ cup coconut milk
- 2 small zucchinis, shredded
- Pepper
- Salt

## Directions:

1. Preheat the oven to 350ºF.
2. Spray casserole dish with cooking spray and set aside.
3. Cook sausage in a pan until brown.
4. Transfer sausage to a mixing bowl.
5. Add coconut flour, milk, eggs, zucchini, pepper, and salt. Stir well.
6. Add eggs and whisk to combine.
7. Transfer bowl mixture into the casserole dish and top with tomato slices.
8. Bake for 50 minutes.
9. Serve and enjoy.

## Nutrition:

Calories 305 Fat 21.8g Carbohydrates 6.3g Sugar 3.3g Protein 19.6g Cholesterol 286mg

## 9.  FRENCH TOAST WITH APPLESAUCE

Preparation Time: 5 minutes
Cooking Time: 15 minutes
Servings: 6
Ingredients:

- ¼ cup unsweetened applesauce
- ½ cup milk
- 1 teaspoons ground cinnamon
- 2 eggs
- 4 tablespoons stevia
- 6 slices whole wheat bread

## Directions:

1. Mix well applesauce, stevia, cinnamon, milk, and eggs in a mixing bowl.
2. Dip the bread into applesauce mixture until wet; take note that you should do this one slice at a time.
3. On medium fire, heat a nonstick skillet greased with cooking spray.
4. Add soaked bread one at a time and cook for 2-3 minutes per side or until lightly browned. Serve and enjoy.

## Nutrition:

Calories: 57 Carbs: 6g Protein: 4g Fats: 4g Phosphorus: 69mg Potassium: 88mg Sodium: 43mg

## 10.  BAGELS MADE HEALTHY

Preparation Time: 5 minutes

**Cooking Time:** 25 minutes
**Servings:** 8
**Ingredients:**

- 2 teaspoons yeast
- 1 ½ tablespoon olive oil
- 1 ¼ cups bread flour
- 2 cups whole wheat flour
- 1 tablespoon vinegar
- 2 tablespoons honey
- 1 ½ cups warm water

**Directions:**

1. In a bread machine, mix all the ingredients, and then process on dough cycle.
2. Once done or end of the cycle, create 8 pieces shaped like a flattened ball.
3. Using your thumb, you must create a hole at the center of each, and then create a donut shape.
4. Place the donut-shaped dough on a greased baking sheet, then covers and let it rise about ½ hour.
5. Prepare about 2 inches of water to boil in a large pan.
6. In boiling water, drop one at a time the bagels and boil for 1 minute, then turn them once.
7. Remove them and return them to a baking sheet and bake at 350oF (175oC) for about 20 to 25 minutes until golden brown.

**Nutrition:**

Calories: 221 Carbs: 42g Protein: 7g Fats: 3g Phosphorus: 130mg Potassium: 166mg Sodium: 47mg

## 11. CORNBREAD WITH SOUTHERN TWIST

**Preparation Time:** 15 minutes
**Cooking Time:** 60 minutes
**Servings:** 8
**Ingredients:**

- 2 tablespoons shortening
- 1 ¼ cups skim milk
- ¼ cup egg substitute
- 4 tablespoons sodium-free baking powder
- ½ cup flour
- 1 ½ cups cornmeal

**Directions:**

1. Prepare an 8x8-inch baking dish or a black iron skillet, and then add shortening.
2. Put the baking dish or skillet inside the oven at 425 ºF; once the shortening has melted, that means the pan is hot already.
3. In a bowl, add milk and egg, and then mix well.
4. Take out the skillet, and add the melted shortening into the batter and stir well.
5. Pour mixture into skillet after mixing all the ingredients.
6. Cook the cornbread for 15-20 minutes until it is golden brown.

**Nutrition:**

Calories: 166 Carbs: 35g Protein: 5g Fats: 1g Phosphorus: 79mg Potassium: 122mg Sodium: 34mg

## 12. GRANDMA'S PANCAKE SPECIAL

**Preparation Time:** 5 minutes
**Cooking Time:** 15 minutes
**Servings:** 3
**Ingredients:**

- 1 tablespoon oil
- 1 cup milk
- 1 egg
- 2 teaspoons sodium-free baking powder
- 4 tablespoons stevia
- 1 ¼ cups flour

**Directions:**

1. Mix together all the dry ingredients, such as the flour, stevia, and baking powder.
2. Combine oil, milk, and egg in another bowl. Once done, add them all to the flour mixture.
3. Make sure that as you stir the mixture; blend them together until slightly lumpy.
4. In a hot, greased griddle, pour-in at least ¼ cup of the batter to make each pancake.
5. To cook, ensure that the bottom is a bit brown, then turn and cook the other side as well.

**Nutrition:**

Calories: 167 Carbs: 50g Protein: 11g Fats: 11g Phosphorus: 176mg Potassium: 215mg Sodium: 70mg

## 13. VERY BERRY SMOOTHIE

**Preparation Time:** 3 minutes
**Cooking Time:** 5 minutes
**Servings:** 2
**Ingredients:**

- 2 quarts water
- 1 cup blackberries
- 1 cup blueberries

**Directions:**

1. Mix all the Ingredients in a blender.
2. Puree until smooth and creamy.
3. Transfer to a serving glass and enjoy.

**Nutrition:**

Calories: 464 Carbs: 111g Protein: 8g Fats: 4g Phosphorus: 132mg Potassium: 843mg Sodium: 16mg

## 14. PASTA WITH INDIAN LENTILS

**Preparation Time:** 5 minutes
**Cooking Time:** 10 minutes
**Servings:** 6
**Ingredients:**

- ¼-½ cup fresh cilantro (chopped)
- 3 cups water
- 2 small dry red peppers (whole)
- 1 teaspoons turmeric
- 1 teaspoons ground cumin
- 2-3 cloves garlic (minced)
- 1 large onion (chopped)
- ½ cup dry lentils (rinsed)
- ½ cup orzo or tiny pasta

**Directions:**

1. Combine all the ingredients in the skillet except for the cilantro, and then boil on medium-high heat.
2. Ensure to cover and slightly reduce heat to medium-low and simmer until pasta is tender for about 35 minutes.
3. Afterwards, take out the chili peppers, then add cilantro and top it with low-fat sour cream.

**Nutrition:**

Calories: 175 Carbs: 40g Protein: 3g Fats: 2g Phosphorus: 139mg Potassium: 513mg Sodium: 61mg

## 15. MEXICAN SCRAMBLED EGGS IN TORTILLA

**Preparation Time:** 5 minutes
**Cooking Time:** 2 minutes
**Servings:** 2
**Ingredients:**

- 2 medium corn tortillas
- 4 egg whites
- 1 teaspoons cumin
- 3 teaspoons green chilies, diced
- ½ teaspoons hot pepper sauce
- 2 tablespoons salsa
- ½ teaspoons salt

**Directions:**

1. Spray some cooking spray on a medium skillet and heat for a few seconds.
2. Whisk the eggs with the green chilies, hot sauce, and comminute
3. Add the eggs into the pan, and whisk with a spatula to scramble. Add the salt.
4. Cook until fluffy and done (1-2 minutes) over low heat.
5. Open the tortillas and spread 1 tablespoon salsa on each.
6. Distribute the egg mixture onto the tortillas and wrap gently to make a burrito.
7. Serve warm.

**Nutrition:**

Calories: 44.1 kcal Carbohydrate: 2.23 g Protein: 7.69 g Sodium: 854 mg Potassium: 189 mg

## 16. RASPBERRY OVERNIGHT PORRIDGE

**Preparation Time:** overnight
**Cooking Time:** 0 minute
**Servings:** 12
**Ingredients:**

- 1/3 cup rolled oats
- ½ cup almond milk
- 1 tablespoon honey
- 5-6 raspberries, fresh or canned and unsweetened
- 1/3 cup rolled oats
- ½ cup almond milk
- 1 tablespoon honey
- 5-6 raspberries, fresh or canned and unsweetened

## Directions:

1. Combine the oats, almond milk, and honey in a mason jar and place into the fridge for overnight.
2. Serve the next morning with the raspberries on top.

## Nutrition:

Calories: 143.6 Kcal Carbohydrate: 34.62 G Protein: 3.44 G Sodium: 77.88 Mg Potassium: 153.25 Mg Phosphorus: 99.3 Mg Dietary Fiber: 7.56 G Fat: 3.91 G

## 17.  AMERICAN BLUEBERRY PANCAKES

**Preparation time:** 5 minutes
**Cooking time:** 10 minutes
**Servings:** 6
**Ingredients**

- 1 ½ cups of all-purpose flour, sifted
- 1 cup of oilmilk
- 3 tablespoons of sugar
- 2 tablespoons of unsalted oil, melted
- 2 teaspoon of baking powder
- 2 eggs, beaten
- 1 cup of canned blueberries, rinsed

## Directions

1. Combine the baking powder, flour and sugar in a bowl.
2. Make a hole in the center and slowly add the rest of the ingredients.
3. Begin to stir gently from the sides to the center with a spatula, until you get a smooth and creamy batter.
4. With cooking spray, spray the pan and place over medium heat.
5. Take one measuring cup and fill 1/3rd of its capacity with the batter to make each pancake.
6. Use a spoon to pour the pancake batter and let cook until golden brown. Flip once to cook the other side.
7. Serve warm with optional agave syrup.

## Nutrition:

Calories: 251.69 kcal carbohydrate: 41.68 g protein: 7.2 g sodium: 186.68 mg potassium: 142.87 mg phosphorus: 255.39 mg dietary fiber: 1.9 g fat: 6.47 g

## 18.  RASPBERRY PEACH BREAKFAST SMOOTHIE

**Preparation time:** 5 minutes

**Cooking time:** 1 minute
**Servings:** 2
**Ingredients**

- 1/3 cup of raspberries, (it can be frozen)
- 1/2 peach, skin and pit removed
- 1 tablespoon of honey
- 1 cup of coconut water

## Directions

1. Mix all ingredients together and blend it until smooth.
2. Pour and serve chilled in a tall glass or mason jar.

## Nutrition:

Calories: 86.3 kcal carbohydrate: 20.6 g protein: 1.4 g sodium: 3 mg potassium: 109 mg phosphorus: 36.08 mg dietary fiber: 2.6 g fat: 0.31 g

## 19.  FAST MICROWAVE EGG SCRAMBLE

**Preparation time:** 5 minutes
**Cooking time:** 1-2 minutes
**Servings:** 1
**Ingredients**

- 1 large egg
- 2 large egg whites
- 2 tablespoons of milk
- Kosher pepper, ground

## Directions

1. Spray a coffee cup with a bit of cooking spray.
2. Whisk all the ingredients together and place into the coffee cup.
3. Place the cup with the eggs into the microwave and set to cook for approx. 45 seconds. Take out and stir.
4. Cook it for another 30 seconds after returning it to the microwave.
5. Serve.

## Nutrition:

Calories: 128.6 kcal Carbohydrate: 2.47 g Protein: 12.96 g Sodium: 286.36 mg Potassium: 185.28 mg Phosphorus: 122.22 mg Dietary fiber: 0 g fat: 5.96 g

## 20.  MANGO LASSI SMOOTHIE

**Preparation time:** 5 minutes
**Cooking time:** 0 minute
**Servings:** 2

## Ingredients

- ½ cup of plain yogurt
- ½ cup of plain water
- ½ cup of sliced mango
- 1 tablespoon of sugar
- ¼ teaspoon of cardamom
- ¼ teaspoon cinnamon
- ¼ cup lime juice

## Directions

1. Pulse all the above ingredients in a blender until smooth (around 1 minute).
2. Pour into tall glasses or mason jars and serve chilled immediately.

## Nutrition:

Calories: 89.02 kcal Carbohydrate: 14.31 g Protein: 2.54 g Sodium: 30 mg Potassium: 185.67 mg Phosphorus: 67.88 mg Dietary Fiber: 0.77 g fat: 2.05 g

## 21. BREAKFAST MAPLE SAUSAGE

**Preparation time:** 15 minutes
**Cooking time:** 8 minutes
**Servings:** 12

## Ingredients

- 1 pound of pork, minced
- ½ pound lean turkey meat, ground
- ¼ teaspoon of nutmeg
- ½ teaspoon black pepper
- ¼ all spice
- 2 tablespoon of maple syrup
- 1 tablespoon of water

## Directions

1. Combine all the ingredients in a bowl.
2. Cover and refrigerate for 3-4 hours.
3. Take the mixture and form into small flat patties with your hand (around 10-12 patties).
4. Lightly grease a medium skillet with oil and shallow fry the patties over medium to high heat, until brown (around 4-5 minutes on each side).
5. Serve hot.

## Nutrition:

Calories: 53.85 kcal Carbohydrate: 2.42 g Protein: 8.5 g Sodium: 30.96 mg Potassium: 84.68 mg Phosphorus: 83.49 mg Dietary fiber: 0.03 g Fat: 0.9 g

## 22. SUMMER VEGGIE OMELET

**Preparation time:** 5 minutes
**Cooking time:** 5 minutes
**Servings:** 2

## Ingredients

- 4 large egg whites
- ¼ cup of sweet corn, frozen
- 1/3 cup of zucchini, grated
- 2 green onions, sliced
- 1 tablespoon of cream cheese
- Kosher pepper

## Directions

1. Grease a medium pan with some cooking spray and add the onions, corn and grated zucchini.
2. Sauté for a couple of minutes until softened.
3. Beat the eggs together with the water, cream cheese, and pepper in a bowl.
4. Add the eggs into the veggie mixture in the pan, and let cook while moving the edges from inside to outside with a spatula, to allow raw egg to cook through the edges.
5. Turn the omelet with the aid of a dish (placed over the pan and flipped upside down and then back to the pan).
6. Let sit for another 1-2 minutes.
7. Fold in half and serve.

## Nutrition:

Calories: 90 kcal Carbohydrate: 15.97 g Protein: 8.07 g Sodium: 227 mg Potassium: 244.24 mg Phosphorus: 45.32 mg Dietary fiber: 0.88 g Fat: 2.44 g

## 23. RASPBERRY OVERNIGHT PORRIDGE

**Preparation time:** overnight
**Cooking time:** 0 minute
**Servings:** 12

## Ingredients

- 1/3 cup of rolled oats
- ½ cup almond milk
- 1 tablespoon of honey
- 5-6 raspberries, fresh or canned and unsweetened

- 1/3 cup of rolled oats
- ½ cup almond milk
- 1 tablespoon of honey
- 5-6 raspberries, fresh or canned and unsweetened

## Directions

1. Combine the oats, almond milk, and honey in a mason jar and place into the fridge for overnight.
2. Serve the next morning with the raspberries on top.

## Nutrition:

Calories: 143.6 kcal carbohydrate: 34.62 g Protein: 3.44 g sodium: 77.88 mg Potassium: 153.25 mg Phosphorus: 99.3 mg Dietary fiber: 7.56 g fat: 3.91 g

## 24. BROCCOLI RICE GRATIN (ITALIAN STYLE)

**Preparation Time:** 30 minutes
**Cooking Time:** 47 minutes
**Serving:** 2
**Ingredients:**

- 125 g (10-minute rice
- salt
- 300 g broccoli florets
- salt
- from the mill: pepper
- 1 teaspoon dried Italian herb
- 1 teaspoon (noble sweet variety) paprika powder
- 125 g (8.5% fat) small mozzarella balls
- 2 tbsp pine nuts
- some basil leaves

## Direction:

1. Following the directions on the packet, cook the rice with plenty of salted water. Meanwhile, clean the broccoli florets and wash them, and cut them into smaller pieces. Add the broccoli to the rice about 5 minutes before cooking time ends, bring it all to a boil again, and simultaneously cook the broccoli.
2. Set the oven to 220 ° C. Brush baking dish (20 x 30 cm approx.) with oil. Drain in a colander with the rice and broccoli and drain. Use salt, pepper, Italian herbs, and paprika powder to season the bell pepper. Mix and dissolve in the baking dish with the broccoli rice mix.
3. Rinse and chop cherry bell pepper in half. Halve the balls of mozzarella as well. Combine the bell pepper and moz-

zarella, sprinkle with the pine nuts, and spread on the broccoli-rice mix. On the middle rack, bake the gratin in the oven for about 10 minutes. To serve, sprinkle with the basil leaves.

## Nutrition:

320 calories 18g protein 45mg potassium 142mg sodium

## 25. BAKED CURRIED APPLE OATMEAL CUPS
by *Carla J. Johnson — Daly City*

**Preparation time:**

10 minutes

**Cooking time:**

20 minutes

**Servings:**

6

## Ingredients

- 3½ cups old-fashioned oats
- 3 tablespoons brown sugar
- 2 teaspoons of your preferred curry powder
- 1/8 teaspoon salt
- 1 cup unsweetened almond milk
- 1 cup unsweetened applesauce
- 1 teaspoon vanilla
- ½ cup chopped walnuts

## Directions

1. Preheat the oven to 375°f. Then spray a 12-cup muffin tin with baking spray then set aside.
2. Combine the oats, brown sugar, curry powder, and salt, and mix in a medium bowl.
3. Mix together the milk, applesauce, and vanilla in a small bowl,
4. Stir the liquid ingredients into the dry ingredients and mix until just combined. Stir in the walnuts.
5. Using a scant 1/3 cup for each divide the mixture among the muffin cups.
6. Bake this for 18 to 20 minutes until the oatmeal is firm. Serve.

## Nutrition:

Calories: 296; total fat: 10g; saturated fat: 1g; sodium: 84mg; phosphorus: 236mg; potassium: 289mg; carbohydrates: 45g; fiber: 6g; protein: 8g; sugar: 11g

## 26. FETA MINT OMELETTE
by Aubrey Ray – Corpus Christi

Preparation Time: 10 minutes
Cooking Time: 5 minutes
Servings: 1

### Ingredients:

- 3 eggs
- 1/4 cup fresh mint, chopped
- 2 tbsp coconut milk
- 1/2 tsp olive oil
- 2 tbsp feta cheese, crumbled
- Pepper
- Salt

### Directions:

1. In a bowl, whisk eggs with feta cheese, mint, milk, pepper, and salt.
2. Heat olive oil in a pan over low heat.
3. Pour egg mixture in the pan and cook until eggs are set.
4. Flip omelet and cook for 2 minutes more.
5. Serve and enjoy.

### Nutrition:

Calories 275 Fat 20 g Carbohydrates 4 g Sugar 2 g Protein 20 g Cholesterol 505 mg phosphorus: 215mg potassium: 269mg sodium: 360mg protein: 19g

## 27. CHERRY BERRY BULGUR BOWL
by James Cole – San Diego

Preparation time: 15 minutes
Cooking time: 15 minutes
Servings: 4

### Ingredients

- 1 cup medium-grind bulgur
- 2 cups water
- Pinch salt
- 1 cup halved and pitted cherries or 1 cup canned cherries, drained
- ½ cup raspberries
- ½ cup blackberries
- 1 tablespoon cherry jam
- 2 cups plain whole-milk yogurt

### Directions

1. Mix the bulgur, water, and salt in a medium saucepan. Do this in a medium heat. Bring to a boil.
2. Reduce the heat to low and simmer, partially covered, for 12 to 15 minutes or until the bulgur is almost tender. Cover, and let stand for 5 minutes to finish cooking do this after removing the pan from the heat.
3. While the bulgur is cooking, combine the raspberries and blackberries in a medium bowl. Stir the cherry jam into the fruit.
4. When the bulgur is tender, divide among four bowls. Top each bowl with ½ cup of yogurt and an equal amount of the berry mixture and serve.

### Nutrition per serving:

Calories: 242; total fat: 6g; saturated fat: 3g; sodium: 85mg; phosphorus: 237mg; potassium: 438mg; carbohydrates: 44g; fiber: 7g; protein: 9g; sugar: 13g

## 28. SAUSAGE CHEESE BAKE OMELETTE
by Ellen Delgado – Wayne

Preparation Time: 10 minutes
Cooking Time: 45 minutes
Servings: 8

### Ingredients:

- 16 eggs
- 2 cups cheddar cheese, shredded
- 1/2 cup salsa
- 1 lb ground sausage
- 1 1/2 cups coconut milk
- Pepper
- Salt

### Directions:

1. Preheat the oven to 350 F.
2. Add sausage in a pan and cook until browned. Drain excess fat.
3. In a large bowl, whisk eggs and milk. Stir in cheese, cooked sausage, and salsa.
4. Pour omelet mixture into the baking dish and bake for 45 minutes.
5. Serve and enjoy.

### Nutrition:

Calories 360 Fat 24 g Carbohydrates 4 g Sugar 3 g Protein 28 g Cholesterol 400 mg  phosphorus: 165mg potassium: 370mg sodium: 135mg

- 2 tablespoons of salsa
- ½ teaspoon salt

## Directions

1. Spray some cooking spray on a medium skillet and heat for a few seconds.
2. Whisk the eggs with the green chilies, hot sauce, and comminute
3. Add the eggs into the pan, and whisk with a spatula to scramble. Add the salt.
4. Cook until fluffy and done (1-2 minutes) over low heat.
5. Open the tortillas and spread 1 tablespoon of salsa on each.
6. Distribute the egg mixture onto the tortillas and wrap gently to make a burrito.
7. Serve warm.

### Nutrition:
Calories: 44.1 kcal carbohydrate: 2.23 g protein: 7.69 g sodium: 854 mg potassium: 189 mg phosphorus: 22 mg dietary fiber: 0.5 g fat: 0.39 g

## 29. ITALIAN BREAKFAST FRITTATA
by Lindsey Youngs – San Francisco

**Preparation Time:** 10 minutes
**Cooking Time:** 45 minutes
**Servings:** 4

### Ingredients:
- 2 cups egg whites
- 1/2 cup mozzarella cheese, shredded
- 1 cup cottage cheese, crumbled
- 1/4 cup fresh basil, sliced
- 1/2 cup roasted red peppers, sliced
- Pepper
- Salt

### Directions:
1. Preheat the oven to 375 F.
2. Add all ingredients into the large bowl and whisk well to combine.
3. Pour frittata mixture into the baking dish and bake for 45 minutes.
4. Slice and serve.

### Nutrition:
Calories 131 Fat 2 g Carbohydrates 5 g Sugar 2 g Protein 22 g Cholesterol 6 mg  phosphorus: 110mg potassium: 117mg sodium: 75mg protein: 7g

## 30. MEXICAN SCRAMBLED EGGS IN TORTILLA
by Evelyn Lechuga – New York

**Preparation time:** 5 minutes
**Cooking time:** 2 minutes
**Servings:** 2

### Ingredients
- 2 medium corn tortillas
- 4 egg whites
- 1 teaspoon of cumin
- 3 teaspoons of green chilies, diced
- ½ teaspoon of hot pepper sauce

# CHAPTER 9
## SOUPS AND STEWS

BE PART OF THIS COMMUNITY OF CRAZY INNOVATORS AND SHARE
YOUR UNCONVENTIONAL KNOWLEDGE...BE PART OF ...
FUN CLUB KITCHEN

## 31. GREEN BEAN VEGGIE STEW

**Preparation Time:** 10 minutes
**Cooking Time:** 30-35 minutes
**Serving:** 1
**Ingredients:**

- 6 cups shredded green cabbage
- 3 celery stalks, chopped
- 1 teaspoon oil
- ½ large sweet onion, chopped
- 1 teaspoon minced garlic
- 1 scallion, chopped
- 2 tablespoons chopped fresh parsley
- 2 tablespoons lemon juice
- 1 teaspoon chopped fresh oregano
- 1 tablespoon chopped fresh thyme
- 1 teaspoon chopped savory
- Water
- 1 cup fresh green beans, cut into 1-inch pieces
- Black pepper (ground), to taste

**Directions:**

1. Take a medium-large cooking pot, heat oil over medium heat.
2. Add onion and stir-cook until it becomes translucent and soft.
3. Add garlic and stir-cook until it becomes fragrant.
4. Add cabbage, celery, scallion, parsley, lemon juice, thyme, savory, and oregano; add water to cover veggies by 3-4 inches.
5. Stir the mixture and boil it.
6. Over low heat, cover, and simmer the mixture for about 25 minutes until veggies are tender.
7. Add green beans and cook for 2-3 more minutes. Season with black pepper to taste. Serve warm.

**Nutrition (Per Serving):**

Calories: 56; Fat: 1g; Phosphorus: 36mg Potassium: 194mg Sodium: 31mg Carbohydrates: 7g Protein: 1g.

## 32. CABBAGE TURKEY SOUP

**Preparation Time:** 10 minutes
**Cooking Time:** 40-45 minutes

**Serving:** 1
**Ingredients:**

- ½ cup shredded green cabbage
- ½ cup bulgur
- 2 dried bay leaves
- 2 tablespoons chopped fresh parsley
- 1 teaspoon chopped fresh sage
- 1 teaspoon chopped fresh thyme
- 1 celery stalk, chopped
- 1 carrot, sliced thin
- ½ sweet onion, chopped
- 1 teaspoon minced garlic
- 1 teaspoon olive oil
- ½ pound cooked ground turkey, 93% lean
- 4 cups water
- 1 cup chicken stock
- Pinch red pepper flakes
- Black pepper (ground), to taste

**Directions:**

1. Take a large saucepan or cooking pot, add oil. Heat over medium heat.
2. Add turkey and stir-cook for 4-5 minutes until evenly brown.
3. Add onion and garlic and sauté for about 3 minutes to soften veggies.
4. Add water, chicken stock, cabbage, bulgur, celery, carrot, and bay leaves.
5. Boil the mixture.
6. Over low heat, cover, and simmer the mixture for about 30-35 minutes until bulgur is cooked well and tender.
7. Remove bay leaves. Add parsley, sage, thyme, and red pepper flakes; stir mixture and season with black pepper. Serve warm.

**Nutrition (Per Serving):**

Calories: 83; Fat: 4g; Phosphorus: 91mg Potassium: 185mg Sodium: 63mg Carbohydrates: 2g Protein: 8g.

## 33. CHICKEN FAJITA SOUP

**Preparation Time:** 10 minutes
**Cooking Time:** 6 hours 30 minutes
**Servings:** 2

## Ingredients:

- 2 pounds of boneless skinless chicken breasts
- 1 onion chopped
- 1 green pepper chopped
- 3 garlic cloves minced
- 1 tablespoonoil
- 6 ounces cream cheese
- salt and pepper to taste

## Directions:

1. Add boneless skinless chicken breasts to a slow cooker and cook for 3 hours on high or 6 hours on low in a cup of chicken broth. Season with salt and pepper. When the chicken is done, remove from the slow cooker and shred. (You can strain the leftover broth for the soup.) In a large saucepan fry green pepper, onion, and garlic in 1 table-spoon ofoil until they are translucent (2 to 3 minutes). Mash the cream cheese into the veggies with a spoon so that it will combine smoothly as it melts.

## Nutrition (Per Serving):

Calories: 306kcal Carbohydrates: 8.2gProtein: 26g; Fat: 17gSaturated Fat: 9gCholesterol: 120mg; Sodium: 880mgPotassium: 757mgFiber: 1.6g; Sugar: 3g

## 34.  CREAM OF CHICKEN SOUP

Preparation Time: 10 minutes
Cooking Time: 20 minutes
Servings: 2
Ingredients:

- 2 cups (500 grams) cauliflower florets
- 2/3 cup (157 ml) unsweetened original almond milk
- 1 cup (250 ml) chicken broth
- 1 teaspoon (5 ml) onion powder
- ½ teaspoon (2.5 ml) grey sea salt
- ¼ teaspoon (1.23 ml) garlic powder
- ¼ teaspoon (1.23 ml) freshly ground black pepper
- 1/8 teaspoon (0.61 ml) celery seed (optional)
- 1/8 teaspoon (0.61 ml) dried thyme
- ¼ cup (30 grams) Beef Gelatin

## Directions:

1. Place all ingredients, except cooked chicken and gelatin, in a small saucepan. Cover and bring to a boil over medium heat. Turn heat to low and cook for about 7 to 8 minutes, until cauliflower is softened. Remove from the heat. Add around ½ cup of the hot liquid to a medium-sized bowl using a ladle. Add gelatin, one scoop at a time. Stir until dissolved, then add the next scoop.

2. Serve immediately.

## Nutrition (Per Serving):

Calories: 198Calories from Fat: 62.1Total Fat: 6.9 gSaturated Fat: 1.1 gCholesterol: 24 mgSodium: 672 mgPhosphorus: 36mPotassium: 194mgCarbs: 9.4 g Dietary Fiber: 3.8 gNet Carbs: 5.6 g Sugars: 3.3 g Protein: 26.4 g.

## 35.  TURKEY & LEMON-GRASS SOUP

Preparation Time: 5 minutes
Cooking Time: 40 minutes
Serving: 1
Ingredients:

- 1 fresh lime
- ¼ cup fresh basil leaves
- 1 tablespoon cilantro
- 1 cup canned and drained water chestnuts
- 1 tablespoon coconut oil
- 1 thumb-size minced ginger piece
- 2 chopped scallions
- 1 finely chopped green chili
- 4 oz. skinless and sliced turkey breasts
- 1 minced garlic clove
- ½ finely sliced stick lemongrass
- 1 chopped white onion
- 4 cups water

## Directions:

1. Crush the lemongrass, cilantro, chili, 1 tablespoon oil, and basil leaves in a blender or with the help of a pestle and mortar, to form a paste. Keep it aside.

2. Heat a large pan/wok with 1 tablespoon olive oil on high heat.

3. Sauté the onions, garlic, and ginger until soft.

4. Add the turkey and brown each side for 4-5 minutes.

5. Add the broth and stir.

6. Now add the prepared paste and stir.

7. Next, add the water chestnuts, turn down the heat slightly and allow it to simmer for 25-30 minutes or until turkey is thoroughly cooked through.

8. Serve hot with the green onion sprinkled over the top.

## Nutrition (Per Serving):

Calories 123 Protein 10 gCarbs 12 g Fat 3 g Sodium (Na) 501 mg; Potassium (K) 151 mg Phosphorus 110 mg.

## 36. BEEF STROGANOFF SOUP

**Preparation Time:** 10 minutes
**Cooking Time:** 30 minutes
**Servings:** 4
**Ingredients:**

- 2 large beef rump (sirloin) steaks (800 g/ 1.76 lbs.)
- 600 g brown or white mushrooms (1.3 lbs.)
- ¼ cup ghee or lard (55 g/ 1.9 oz.)
- 2 cloves garlic, minced
- 1 medium white or brown onion, chopped (110 g/ 3.9 oz.)
- 5 cups bone broth or chicken stock or vegetable stock (1.2 l/ quart)
- 2 tsps. paprika
- 1 tbsp of Dijon mustard (you can make your own)
- Juice from 1 lemon (~ 4 tbsp.)
- 1½ cup sour cream or heavy whipping cream (345 g/ 12.2 oz.) - you can use paleo-friendly coconut cream
- ¼ cup freshly chopped parsley
- 1 tsp salt
- ¼ tsp freshly ground black pepper

## Directions:

1. Lay the steaks in the freezer in a single layer for 30 to 45 minutes.
2. This will make it easy to slice the steaks into thin strips. Meanwhile, clean and slice the mushrooms.
3. Fry over a medium-high heat until they're cooked through and browned from all sides. Remove the slices from the pan and place them in a bowl. Set aside for later. Do the same for the remaining slices.
4. Grease the pan with the remaining ghee. Add in the chopped onion and minced garlic to the pan and cook until lightly browned and fragrant.
5. Add the sliced mushrooms and cook for 3 to 4 more minutes while stirring occasionally. Then add your Dijon mustard, paprika, and pour in the bone broth. Add lemon juice and boil for 2 to 3 minutes. Add the browned beef slices and sour cream. Remove from heat. If you are using

a thickener, add it to the pot and stir well. Finally, add freshly chopped parsley. Eat hot with a slice of toasted Keto Bread or let it cool down and store in the fridge for up to 5 days. Enjoy!

## Nutrition:

Calories from carbs 7% protein 27%, fat 66 Total carbs 10.8 g Fiber 1.4 gram Sugars 4.8 grams Saturated fat 18.4 grams Sodium 783 mg (34% RDA Potassium 1,398 mg (70% EMR).

## 37. GREEN CHICKEN ENCHILADA SOUP

**Preparation Time:** 10 minutes
**Cooking Time:** 5 minutes
**Servings** 6
**Ingredients:**

- ½ cup salsa Verde
- 4 ounces cream cheese, softened
- 1 cup sharp cheddar cheese, shredded
- 2 cups bone broth or chicken stock
- 2 cups cooked chicken, shredded

## Direction:

1. Add the salsa, cream cheese, cheddar cheese and chicken stock in a blender and blend until smooth. Pour into a medium saucepan and cook on medium until hot.

## Nutrition:

Calories 346Fat 22Carbohydrates 3g netProtein 32g

## 38. MEDITERRANEAN VEGETABLE SOUP

**Preparation Time:** 5 minutes
**Cooking Time:** 30 minutes
**Servings:** 4
**Ingredients:**

- 1 tbsp. oregano
- 2 minced garlic cloves
- 1 tsp. black pepper
- 1 diced zucchini
- 1 cup diced eggplant
- 4 cups water
- 1 diced red pepper
- 1 tbsp. extra-virgin olive oil
- 1 diced red onion

## Directions:

1. Soak the vegetables in warm water prior to use.
2. In a large pot, add the oil, chopped onion and minced garlic.
3. Simmer for 5 minutes on low heat.
4. Add the other vegetables to the onions and cook for 7-8 minutes.
5. Add the stock to the pan and bring to a boil on high heat.
6. Stir in the herbs, reduce the heat, and simmer for a further 20 minutes or until thoroughly cooked through.
7. Season with pepper to serve.

## Nutrition:

Calories 152 Protein 1g Carbs 6g Fat 3g Sodium (Na) 3mg Potassium (K) 229mg Phosphorus 45mg

## 39. TOFU SOUP

Preparation Time: 5 minutes
Cooking Time: 10 minutes
Servings: 2

## Ingredients:

- 1 tbsp. miso paste
- 1/8 cup cubed soft tofu
- 1 chopped green onion
- ¼ cup sliced Shiitake mushrooms
- 3 cups Renali stock
- 1 tbsp. soy sauce

## Directions:

1. In a saucepan, boil the stock on high heat. Reduce heat to medium and let it simmer. Add mushrooms and cook for another 3 minutes.
2. Mix Soy sauce (reduced salt) and miso paste in a bowl. Add this mixture and the tofu to the stock. Simmer for nearly 5 minutes and serve with chopped green onion.

## Nutrition:

Calories 129 Fat 7.8g Sodium (Na) 484mg Potassium (K) 435mg Protein 11g Carbs 5.5g Phosphorus 73.2mg

## 40. COFFEE AND WINE BEEF STEW

Preparation Time: 20 minutes
Cooking Time: 3 hours and 20 minutes
Servings: 6

## Ingredients:

- Pounds Stew Meat
- 3 c. Coffee
- 1 c. Beef Stock
- 2 tbsp. Capers
- 2 tsp. Garlic
- 1 tsp. Salt
- 1 tsp. Pepper

## Directions:

1. Cube all stew meat and thinly slice onions and mushrooms.
2. Heat 3 tablespoons of coconut oil in a pan. Season the beef with salt and pepper, then brown all of it in small batches. Stir mixture well.
3. Add beef into the mixture, bring to a boil then reduce heat to low. Cover and cook for 3 hours. Serve and enjoy.

## Nutrition:

Calories 504 Fats 32.2gNet Carbs 2.7gProtein 42.5g

## 41. BEEF STEW

Preparation Time: 10 minutes
Cooking Time: 1 hour
Servings: 4

## Ingredients:

- 1 pound Beef Short Rib
- 2 cups beef broth
- 4 cloves minced garlic
- 100g onion
- 100g carrot
- 100g radishes
- ¼ tsp Pink Himalayan Salt
- ¼ tsp pepper
- ½ tsp xanthan Gum
- 1 tbspoil
- 1 tbsp coconut oil

## Directions:

1. On medium-high heat, heat a large saucepan and add coconut oil.
2. Then add short rib and brown on all sides. Remove from saucepan and set aside.

3. Chop onions, carrots and radishes into bite sized pieces and mince garlic. Add onions, garlic andoil and cook for a couple of minutes.
4. Once the onions are soft, add the broth and combine.
5. Add the xanthan gum and mix. Allow broth mixture to come to a boil and then transfer the meat back in and cook covered for 30 minutes.
6. Stir frequently scraping the bottom as you stir.
7. After 30 minutes, add the carrots and radishes and cook for 30 more minutes, stirring frequently until it thickens.
8. If you feel the need you can add more broth or some water.
9. Serve warm and enjoy!

## Nutrition:

Calories 432.25kcaCarbohydrates 5.5gProtein 19.25gFat 36.5gFiber 1.5g

## 42. BARBEQUE SAUCE

**Preparation Time:** 5 minutes
**Cooking Time:** 5 minutes
**Servings:** 8 (2 tbsp per serving)
## Ingredients:

- 5 tbsp + 1 tsp canola oil
- ¼ tsp onion powder
- 1 tbsp brown sugar
- ¼ cup vinegar
- 1 tbsp paprika
- ½ cup unsalted tomato juice
- 1 clove garlic (crushed)
- 1/3 cup water
- 1 tsp pepper

## Directions:

1. Combine all the ingredients in a saucepan.
2. Bring the mixture to a boil, reduce the heat and simmer the sauce for 20 minutes.
3. Pour leftover into a tightly sealed container and store in a refrigerator.

## Nutrition:

Calories 95Total Fat 9.4gSodium 3mgTotal Carbohydrate 2.7gProtein 0.3g Calcium 7mgPotassium 68mg

## 43. CHICKEN WILD RICE SOUP

**Preparation Time:** 10 minutes
**Cooking Time:** 15 minutes
**Servings:**
6

## Ingredients:

- 2/3 cup wild rice, uncooked
- 1 tbsp onion, chopped finely
- 1 tbsp fresh parsley, chopped
- 1 cup carrots, chopped
- 8 oz chicken breast, cooked
- 2 tbspoil
- 1/4 cup all-purpose white flour
- 5 cups low-sodium chicken broth
- 1 tbsp slivered almonds

## Direction:

1. Start by adding rice and 2 cups broth along with ½ cup water to a cooking pot.
2. Cook until the rice is al dente and set it aside.
3. Addoil to a saucepan and melt it.
4. Stir in onion and sauté until soft then add the flour and the remaining broth.
5. Stir and cook for 1 minute then add the chicken, cooked rice, and carrots.
6. Cook for 5 minutes on simmer.
7. Garnish with almonds. Serve fresh.

## Nutrition:

Calories 287. Protein 21 g. Carbohydrates 35 g. Fat 7 g. Cholesterol 42 mg. Sodium 182 mg. Potassium 384 mg. Phosphorus 217 mg. Calcium 45 mg. Fiber 1.6 g.

## 44. CHICKEN NOODLE SOUP

**Preparation Time:** 10 minutes
**Cooking Time:** 25 minutes
**Servings:** 2
## Ingredients:

- 1 1/2 cups low-sodium vegetable broth
- 1 cup water
- 1/4 tsp poultry seasoning
- 1/4 tsp black pepper
- 1 cup chicken strips

- 1/4 cup carrot
- 2 oz egg noodles, uncooked

## Directions:

1. Toss all the ingredients into a slow cooker
2. Cook soup on high heat for 25 minutes.
3. Serve warm.

## Nutrition:

Calories 103. Protein 8 g. Carbohydrates 11 g. Fat 3 g. Cholesterol 4 mg. Sodium 355 mg. Potassium 264 mg. Phosphorus 128 mg. Calcium 46 mg. Fiber 4.0 g.

## 45. CUCUMBER SOUP

Preparation Time: 10 minutes
Cooking Time: 0 minutes
Servings: 4

## Ingredients:

- 2 medium cucumbers, peeled and diced
- 1/3 cup sweet white onion, diced
- 1 green onion, diced
- 1/4 cup fresh mint
- 2 tbsp fresh dill
- 2 tbsp lemon juice
- 2/3 cup water
- 1/2 cup half and half cream
- 1/3 cup sour cream
- 1/2 tsp pepper
- Fresh dill sprigs for garnish

## Directions:

1. Toss all the ingredients into a food processor.
2. Puree the mixture and refrigerate for 2 hours.
3. Garnish with dill sprigs.
4. Enjoy fresh.

## Nutrition:

Calories 77. Protein 2 g. Carbohydrates 6 g. Fat 5 g. Cholesterol 12 mg. Sodium 128 mg. Potassium 258 mg. Phosphorus 64 mg. Calcium 60 mg. Fiber 1.0 g.

## 46. SQUASH AND TURMERIC SOUP

Preparation Time: 10 minutes
Cooking Time: 30 minutes

Servings: 4

## Ingredients:

- 4 cups low-sodium vegetable broth
- 2 medium zucchini squash, peeled and diced
- 2 medium yellow crookneck squash, peeled and diced
- 1 small onion, diced
- 1/2 cup frozen green peas
- 2 tbsp olive oil
- 1/2 cup plain nonfat Greek yogurt
- 2 tsp turmeric

## Directions:

1. Warm the broth in a saucepan on medium heat.
2. Toss in onion, squash, and zucchini.
3. Let it simmer for approximately 25 minutes then add oil and green peas.
4. Cook for another 5 minutes then allow it to cool.
5. Puree the soup using a handheld blender then add Greek yogurt and turmeric.
6. Refrigerate it overnight and serve fresh.

## Nutrition:

Calories 100. Protein 4 g. Carbohydrates 10 g. Fat 5 g. Cholesterol 1 mg. Sodium 279 mg. Potassium 504 mg. Phosphorus 138 mg. Calcium 60 mg. Fiber 2.8 g.

## 47. WILD RICE ASPARAGUS SOUP
by Marion Overstreet – Johnson City

Preparation Time: 10 minutes
Cooking Time: 30 minutes
Servings: 4

## Ingredients:

- 3/4 cup wild rice
- 2 cups asparagus, chopped
- 1 cup carrots, diced
- 1/2 cup onion, diced
- 3 garlic cloves, minced
- 1/4 cup oil
- 1/2 tsp thyme
- 1/2 tsp fresh ground pepper
- 1/4 tsp nutmeg
- 1 bay leaf

- 1/2 cup all-purpose flour
- 4 cups low-sodium chicken broth
- 1/2 cup extra dry vermouth
- 2 cups cooked chicken
- 4 cups unsweetened almond milk, unenriched

## Directions:

1. Cook the wild rice as per the cooking instructions on the box or bag and drain.
2. Melt theoil in a Dutch oven and sauté garlic and onion.
3. Once soft, add spices, herbs, and carrots.
4. Cook on medium heat right until veggies are tender then add flour and stir cook for 10 minutes on low heat.
5. Add 4 cups of broth and vermouth and blend using a hand-held blender.
6. Dice the chicken pieces and add asparagus and chicken to the soup.
7. Stir in almond milk and cook for 20 minutes.
8. Add the wild rice and serve warm.

**Nutrition:**

Calories 295. Protein 21 g. Carbohydrates 28 g. Fat 11 g. Cholesterol 45 mg. Sodium 385 mg. Potassium 527 mg. Phosphorus 252 mg. Calcium 183 mg. Fiber 3.3

## 48. NUTMEG CHICKEN SOUP
by Dorothy Walla – San Antonio

**Preparation Time:** 10 minutes
**Cooking Time:** 20 minutes
**Servings:** 4

### Ingredients:

- 1 lb. boneless, skinless chicken breasts, uncooked
- 1 1/2 cups onion, sliced
- 1 1/2 cups celery, chopped
- 1 tbsp olive oil
- 1 cup fresh carrots, chopped
- 1 cup fresh green beans, chopped
- 3 tbsp all-purpose white flour
- 1 tsp dried oregano
- 2 tsp dried basil
- 1/4 tsp nutmeg
- 1 tsp thyme

- 32 oz reduced-sodium chicken broth
- 1/2 cup 1% low-fat milk
- 2 cups frozen green peas
- 1/4 tsp black pepper

## Directions:

1. Add chicken to a skillet and sauté for 6 minutes then remove it from the heat.
2. Warm up olive oil in a pan and sauté onion for 5 minutes.
3. Stir in green beans, carrots, chicken, basil, oregano, flour, thyme, and nutmeg.
4. Sauté for 3 minutes then transfer the ingredients to a large pan.
5. Add milk and broth and cook until it boils.
6. Stir in green peas and cook for 5 minutes.
7. Adjust seasoning with pepper and serve warm.

**Nutrition:**

Calories 131. Protein 14 g. Carbohydrates 12 g. Fat 3 g. Cholesterol 32 mg. Sodium 343 mg. Potassium 467 mg. Phosphorus 171 mg. Calcium 67 mg. Fiber 2.8 g.

## 49. HUNGARIAN CHERRY SOUP
by Barbara Rice – New York

**Preparation Time:** 10 minutes
**Cooking Time:** 15 minutes
**Servings:** 4

### Ingredients:

- 1 1/2 cup fresh cherries
- 3 cups water
- 2 cups stevia
- 1/16 tsp salt
- 1 tbsp all-purpose white flour
- 1/2 cup reduced-fat sour cream

## Directions:

1. Warm the water in a saucepan and add cherries and stevia.
2. Let it boil then simmer for 10 minutes.
3. Remove 2 tbsp of the cooking liquid and keep it aside.
4. Separate ¼ cup of liquid in a bowl and allow it to cool.
5. Add flour and sour cream to this liquid.

6. Mix well then return the mixture to the saucepan. Cook for 5 minutes on low heat. Garnish the soup with the reserved 2 tbsp of liquid. Serve and enjoy.

**Nutrition:**

Calories 144. Protein 2 g. Carbohydrates 25 g. Fat 4 g. Cholesterol 12 mg. Sodium 57 mg. Potassium 144 mg. Phosphorus 40 mg. Calcium 47 mg. Fiber 1.0 g.

## 50. OXTAIL SOUP
by Robert Wilson — Bakersfield

**Preparation Time:** 10 minutes
**Cooking Time:** 20 minutes
**Servings:** 4

**Ingredients:**

- 1 medium bell pepper, diced
- 1 small jalapeno pepper, diced
- 1 large onion, sliced
- 3 celery stalks, chopped
- 1 tbsp olive oil
- 1 tbsp all-purpose white flour
- 2 bouillon cubes
- 2-lb package oxtail
- 1 tbsp vinegar
- 1/4 tsp black pepper
- 1/2 tsp herb seasoning blend
- 12 oz frozen gumbo vegetables

**Directions:**

1. Start by adding olive oil, flour, and the bouillon cubes to a saucepan.
2. Add water 3/4 of the way up the saucepan and let it boil.
3. Stir in peppers, vinegar, and oxtails.
4. Cover it and cook until the oxtails soften.
5. Add all vegetables including, celery, and onion to the soup.
6. Cook until the veggies soften.
7. Serve fresh and warm.

**Nutrition:**

Calories 313. Protein 21 g. Carbohydrates 10 g. Fat 21 g. Cholesterol 66 mg. Sodium 325 mg. Potassium 596 mg. Phosphorus 257 mg. Calcium 61 mg. Fiber 2.2 g.

## 51. CLASSIC CHICKEN SOUP
by Robert Hartigan — Huntington

**Preparation Time:** 5-10 minutes
**Cooking Time:** 35 minutes
**Serving:** 1

**Ingredients:**

- 2 teaspoons minced garlic
- 2 celery stalks, chopped
- 1 tablespoon oil
- ½ sweet onion, diced
- 1 carrot, diced
- 4 cups water
- 1 teaspoon chopped fresh thyme
- 2 cups chopped cooked chicken breast
- 1 cup chicken stock
- Black pepper (ground), to taste
- 2 tablespoons chopped fresh parsley

**Directions:**

1. Take a medium-large cooking pot, heat oil over medium heat.
2. Add onion and stir-cook until it becomes translucent and softened.
3. Add garlic and stir-cook until it becomes fragrant.
4. Add celery, carrot, chicken, chicken stock, and water. Boil the mixture.
5. Over low heat simmers the mixture for about 25-30 minutes until veggies are tender.
6. Mix in thyme and cook for 2 minutes. Season to taste with black pepper.
7. Serve warm with parsley on top.

Nutrition (Per Serving):

## 52. BEEF OKRA SOUP
by David Dingess – Long Beach

**Preparation Time:** 10 minutes
**Cooking Time:** 45-55 minutes
**Serving:** 1

### Ingredients:

- ½ cup okra
- ½ teaspoon basil
- ½ cup carrots, diced
- 3 ½ cups water
- 1-pound beef stew meat
- 1 cup raw sliced onions
- ½ cup green peas
- 1 teaspoon black pepper
- ½ teaspoon thyme
- ½ cup corn kernels

### Directions:

1. Take a medium-large cooking pot, heat oil over medium heat.
2. Add water, beef stew meat, black pepper, onions, basil, thyme, and stir-cook for 40-45 minutes until meat is tender.
3. Add all veggies. Over low heat simmers the mixture for about 20-25 minutes. Add more water if needed.
4. Serve soup warm.

### Nutrition (Per Serving):

Calories: 187. Fat: 12g. Phosphorus: 119mgPotassium: 288mgSodium: 59mgCarbohydrates: 7g Protein: 11g

# CHAPTER 10
## FISH AND SEAFOOD

## 53. CHILI MUSSELS

Preparation Time: 7 minutes
Cooking Time: 10 minutes
Servings: 4
Ingredients:

- 1-pound mussels
- 1 chili pepper, chopped
- 1 cup chicken stock
- ½ cup milk
- 1 teaspoon olive oil
- 1 teaspoon minced garlic
- 1 teaspoon ground coriander
- ½ teaspoon salt
- 1 cup fresh parsley, chopped
- 4 tablespoons lemon juice

### Directions:

1. Pour milk in the saucepan. Add chili pepper, chicken stock, olive oil, minced garlic, ground coriander, salt, and lemon juice. Bring the liquid to boil and add mussels.
2. Boil the mussel for 4 minutes or until they will open shells. Then add chopped parsley and mix up the meal well. Remove it from the heat.

### Nutrition:

Calories: 136 Fat: 4.7g. Fiber: 0.6g. Carbs: 7.5g. Protein: 15.3g.

## 54. OREGON TUNA PATTIES

Preparation Time: 10 minutes
Cooking Time: 15 minutes
Servings: 4
Ingredients:

- 1 (14.75 ounce) can tuna
- 2 tablespoonsoil
- 1 medium onion, chopped
- 2/3 cup graham cracker crumbs
- 2 egg whites, beaten
- 1/4 cup chopped fresh parsley
- 1 teaspoon dry mustard
- 3 tablespoons olive oil.

### Directions:

1. Drain the tuna, reserving 3/4 cup of the liquid. Flake the meat. Meltoil in a large skillet over medium-high heat. Add onion, and cook until tender. In a medium bowl, combine the onions with the reserved tuna liquid, 1/3 of the graham cracker crumbs, egg whites, parsley, mustard, and tuna.

### Nutrition:

Calories: 204 Sodium: 111mg Protein: 10.5g Potassium: 164mg Phosphorus: 106mg.

## 55. SCRAMBLED EGGS WITH CRAB

Preparation Time: 10 minutes
Cooking Time: 8 minutes
Servings: 4
Ingredients:

- 6 large eggs
- 4 egg whites
- 1/8 Teaspoon freshly ground black pepper
- 2 tablespoons oil
- 1 red bell pepper, chopped
- 3 scallions, white and green parts, chopped
- 1 (6-ounce) can crab meat, drained
- ¼ cup shredded Swiss cheese
- 1 tablespoon chopped fresh chives.

### Directions:

1. In a medium bowl, whisk together the eggs, egg whites, and pepper until well blended and set aside.
2. Melt theoil in a large skillet over medium heat.
3. Sauté the red bell pepper and scallions for 2 minutes. Stir in the crab and cook for 1 minute longer. Remove this mixture from the skillet to a plate and set aside.
4. Add the beaten eggs to the skillet and cook, stirring occasionally, until the eggs form large curds and are set, about 2 to 4 minutes.
5. Add the vegetables and crab back to the eggs. Sprinkle with the cheese and cover the skillet for 1 minute to melt the cheese.
6. Remove the cover, sprinkle with the chives, and serve.

### Nutrition:

Calories: 258 Total fat: 16g Saturated fat: 7g Sodium: 404mg Potassium: 346mg Phosphorus: 285mg.

## 56. SHRIMP PAELLA

**Preparation Time:** 5 minutes
**Cooking Time:** 10 minutes
**Servings:** 2
**Ingredients:**

- 1 cup cooked brown rice
- 1 chopped red onion
- 1 tsp. paprika
- 1 chopped garlic clove
- 1 tbsp. olive oil
- 6 oz. frozen cooked shrimp
- 1 deseeded and sliced chili pepper
- 1 tbsp. oregano.

**Directions:**

1. Heat the olive oil in a large pan on medium-high heat.
2. Add the onion and garlic and sauté for 2-3 minutes until soft.
3. Now add the shrimp and sauté for a further 5 minutes or until hot through.
4. Now add the herbs, spices, chili, and rice with 1/2 cup boiling water.
5. Stir until everything is warm, and the water has been absorbed.
6. Plate up and serve.

**Nutrition:**

Calories: 221 Protein: 17g Sodium: 235mg Potassium: 176mg Phosphorus: 189mg.

## 57. BAKED FENNEL & GARLIC SALMON

**Preparation Time:**

5 minutes
**Cooking Time:**

15 minutes
**Servings:**

2
**Ingredients:**

- 1 lemon
- ½ sliced fennel bulb
- 6 oz. salmon fillets
- 1 tsp. black pepper
- 2 garlic cloves.

**Directions:**

1. Preheat the oven to 375°F/Gas mark 5. Sprinkle black pepper over the Salmon. Slice the fennel bulb and garlic cloves. Add 1 salmon fillet and half the fennel and garlic to one sheet of baking paper or tin foil. Squeeze in 1/2 lemon juices. Repeat for the other fillet. Fold and add to the oven for 12-15 minutes or until fish is thoroughly cooked through.
2. Meanwhile, add boiling water to your couscous, cover, and allow to steam.
3. Serve with your choice of rice or salad.

**Nutrition:**

Calories: 221 Protein: 14g Carbs: 3g Fat: 2g Sodium: 119mg Potassium: 398mg Phosphorus: 149mg.

## 58. OREGANO SEABASS WITH CRUNCHY CRUST

**Preparation Time:** 10 minutes
**Cooking Time:** 2 hours
**Servings:** 2
**Ingredients:**

- 8 oz. salmon fillet
- 2 tablespoons panko breadcrumbs
- 1 oz. Parmesan, grated
- 1 teaspoon dried oregano
- 1 teaspoon sunflower oil.

**Directions:**

1. In the mixing bowl, combine together panko breadcrumbs, Parmesan, and dried oregano. Sprinkle the salmon with olive oil and coat in the breadcrumb's mixture. After this, line the baking tray with baking paper. Place the salmon in the tray and transfer in the preheated to the 385F oven. Bake the salmon for 25 minutes.

**Nutrition:**

Calories: 245 Fat: 12.8g Fiber: 0.6g Carbs: 5.9g Protein: 27.5g.

## 59. SARDINE FISH CAKES

**Preparation Time:** 10 minutes
**Cooking Time:** 10 minutes
**Servings:** 4
**Ingredients:**

- 11 oz. sardines, canned, drained
- 1/3 cup shallot, chopped
- 1 teaspoon chili flakes
- ½ teaspoon salt
- 2 tablespoon wheat flour, whole grain
- 1 egg, beaten
- 1 tablespoon chives, chopped
- 1 teaspoon olive oil
- 1 teaspoonoil.

## Directions:

1. Put theoil in the skillet and melt it.
2. Add shallot and cook it until translucent.
3. After this, transfer the shallot to the mixing bowl.
4. Add sardines, chili flakes, salt, flour, egg, chives, and mix up until smooth with the help of the fork. Make the medium size cakes and place them in the skillet. Add olive oil. Roast the fish cakes for 3 minutes from each side over the medium heat.
5. Dry the cooked fish cakes with the paper towel if needed and transfer to the serving plates.

## Nutrition:

Calories: 221 Fat: 12.2g Fiber: 0.1g Carbs: 5.4g Protein: 21.3g.

## 60. CAJUN CATFISH

Preparation Time: 10 minutes
Cooking Time: 10 minutes
Servings: 4
Ingredients:

- 16 oz. catfish steaks (4 oz. each fish steak)
- 1 tablespoon Cajun spices
- 1 egg, beaten
- 1 tablespoon sunflower oil.

## Directions:

1. Pour sunflower oil into the skillet and preheat it until shimmering. Meanwhile, dip every catfish steak in the beaten egg and coat in Cajun spices. Place the fish steaks in the hot oil and roast them for 4 minutes from each side. The cooked catfish steaks should have a light brown crust.

## Nutrition:

Calories: 263 Fat: 16.7g Fiber: 0g Carbs: 0.1g Protein: 26.3g.

## 61. 4-INGREDIENTS SALMON FILLET

Preparation Time: 5 minutes
Cooking Time: 25 minutes
Servings: 1
Ingredients:

- 4 oz. salmon fillet
- ½ teaspoon salt
- 1 teaspoon sesame oil
- ½ teaspoon sage.

## Directions:

1. Rub the fillet with salt and sage. Place the fish in the tray and sprinkle it with sesame oil. Cook the fish for 25 minutes at 365F. Flip the fish carefully onto another side after 12 minutes of cooking.

## Nutrition:

Calories: 191 Fat: 11.6g Fiber: 0.1g Carbs: 0.2g Protein: 22g.

## 62. SPANISH COD IN SAUCE

Preparation Time: 10 minutes
Cooking Time: 5.5 hours
Servings: 2
Ingredients:

- 1 teaspoon tomato paste
- 1 teaspoon garlic, diced
- 1 white onion, sliced
- 1 jalapeno pepper, chopped
- 1/3 cup chicken stock
- 7 oz. Spanish cod fillet
- 1 teaspoon paprika
- 1 teaspoon salt.

## Directions:

1. Pour chicken stock into the saucepan.
2. Add tomato paste and mix up the liquid until homogenous.
3. Add garlic, onion, jalapeno pepper, paprika, and salt.
4. Bring the liquid to boil and then simmer it.
5. Chop the cod fillet and add it to the tomato liquid.
6. Close the lid and simmer the fish for 10 minutes over the low heat.
7. Serve the fish in the bowls with tomato sauce.

## Nutrition:

Calories: 113 Fat: 1.2g Fiber: 1.9g Carbs: 7.2g Protein: 18.9g.

## 63. FISH SHAKSHUKA

Preparation Time: 5 minutes
Cooking Time: 15 minutes
Servings: 5
Ingredients:

- 5 eggs
- 1 cup tomatoes, chopped
- 3 bell peppers, chopped
- 1 tablespoonoil
- 1 teaspoon tomato paste
- 1 teaspoon chili pepper
- 1 teaspoon salt
- 1 tablespoon fresh dill
- 5 oz. cod fillet, chopped
- 1 tablespoon scallions, chopped.

### Directions:

1. Meltoil in the skillet and add chili pepper, bell peppers, and tomatoes.
2. Sprinkle the vegetables with scallions, dill, salt, and chili pepper. Simmer them for 5 minutes.
3. After this, add chopped cod fillet and mix up well.
4. Close the lid and simmer the Ingredients for 5 minutes over the medium heat.
5. Then crack the eggs over the fish and close the lid.
6. Cook Shakshuka with the closed lid for 5 minutes.

### Nutrition:

Calories: 143 Fat: 7.3g Fiber: 1.6g Carbs: 7.9g Protein: 12.8g.

## 64. SALMON BAKED IN FOIL WITH FRESH THYME

Preparation Time: 10 minutes
Cooking Time: 30 minutes
Servings: 4
Ingredients:

- 4 fresh thyme sprigs
- 4 garlic cloves, peeled, roughly chopped
- 16 oz. salmon fillets (4 oz. each fillet)
- ½ teaspoon salt

- ½ teaspoon ground black pepper
- 4 tablespoons cream
- 4 teaspoonsoil
- ¼ teaspoon cumin seeds.

### Directions:

1. Line the baking tray with foil.
2. Sprinkle the fish fillets with salt, ground black pepper, cumin seeds, and arrange them in the tray with oil.
3. Add thyme sprig on the top of every fillet.
4. Then add cream,oil, and garlic.
5. Bake the fish for 30 minutes at 345F.

### Nutrition:

Calories: 198 Fat: 11.6g Fiber: 0.2g Carbs: 1.8g Protein: 22.4g.

## 65. HADDOCK &OILED LEEKS

Preparation Time: 5 minutes
Cooking Time: 15 minutes
Servings: 2
Ingredients:

- 1 tbsp. oil
- 1 sliced leek
- ¼ tsp. black pepper
- 2 tsp. Chopped parsley
- 6 oz. haddock fillets
- ½ juiced lemon.

### Directions:

1. Preheat the oven to 375°F/Gas Mark 5.
2. Add the haddock fillets to baking or parchment paper and sprinkle with the black pepper.
3. Squeeze over the lemon juice and wrap into a parcel.
4. Bake the parcel on a baking tray for 10-15 minutes or until the fish is thoroughly cooked through.
5. Meanwhile, heat theoil over medium-low heat in a small pan.
6. Add the leeks and parsley and sauté for 5-7 minutes until soft.
7. Serve the haddock fillets on a bed ofoiled leeks and enjoy!

### Nutrition:

Calories: 124 Protein: 15g Carbs: 0g Fat: 7g Sodium: 161mg Potassium: 251mg Phosphorus: 220mg.

## 66. THAI SPICED HALIBUT

**Preparation Time:** 5 minutes
**Cooking Time:** 20 minutes
**Servings:** 2
**Ingredients:**

- 2 tbsps. coconut oil
- 1 cup white rice
- ¼ tsp. black pepper
- ½ diced red chili
- 1 tbsp. fresh basil
- 2 pressed garlic cloves
- 4 oz. halibut fillet
- 1 halved lime
- 2 sliced green onions
- 1 lime leaf.

**Directions:**

1. Preheat oven to 400°F/Gas Mark 5.
2. Add half of the Ingredients into baking paper and fold into a parcel.
3. Repeat for your second parcel.
4. Add to the oven for 15-20 minutes or until fish is thoroughly cooked through.
5. Serve with cooked rice.

**Nutrition:**

Calories: 311 Protein: 16g Carbs: 17g Fat: 15g Sodium: 31mg Potassium: 418mg Phosphorus: 257mg.

## 67. MONKFISH CURRY
by James McClendon – Minneapolis

**Preparation Time:** 5 minutes
**Cooking Time:** 20 minutes
**Servings:** 2
**Ingredients:**

- 1 garlic clove
- 3 finely chopped green onions
- 1 tsp. grated ginger
- 1 cup water
- 2 tsp. chopped fresh basil
- 1 cup cooked rice noodles
- 1 tbsp. coconut oil
- ½ sliced red chili
- 4 oz. monkfish fillet
- ½ finely sliced stick lemon-grass
- 2 tbsps. chopped shallots.

**Directions:**

1. Slice the monkfish into bite-size pieces.
2. Using a pestle and mortar or food processor, crush the basil, garlic, ginger, chili, and lemon-grass to form a paste.
3. Heat the oil in a large wok or pan over medium-high heat and add the shallots.
4. Now add the water to the pan and bring to the boil.
5. Add the monkfish, lower the heat and cover to simmer for 10 minutes or until cooked through. Enjoy with rice noodles and scatter with green onions to serve.

**Nutrition:**

Calories: 249 Protein: 12g Carbs: 30g Fat: 10g Sodium: 32mg Potassium: 398mg Phosphorus: 190mg.

## 68. TUNA CASSEROLE
by Michael McLain – Bensenville

**Preparation Time:** 15 minutes
**Cooking Time:** 35 minutes
**Servings:** 4
**Ingredients:**

- ½ cup cheddar cheese, shredded
- 2 tomatoes, chopped
- 7 oz. tuna filet, chopped
- 1 teaspoon ground coriander
- ½ teaspoon salt
- 1 teaspoon olive oil
- ½ teaspoon dried oregano.

**Directions:**

1. Brush the casserole mold with olive oil.
2. Mix up together chopped tuna fillet with dried oregano and ground coriander.
3. Place the fish in the mold and flatten well to get the layer.
4. Then add shredded cheese.
5. Cover the casserole with foil and secure the edges.
6. Bake the meal for 35 minutes at 355F.

**Nutrition:**
Calories: 260 Fat: 21.5g Fiber: 0.8g Carbs: 2.7g. Protein: 14.6g.

## 69. FISH CHILI WITH LENTILS
by Thomas J. Bradley – Fairbanks

**Preparation Time:** 10 minutes
**Cooking Time:** 30 minutes
**Servings:** 4
**Ingredients:**

- 1 red pepper, chopped
- 1 yellow onion, diced
- 1 teaspoon ground black pepper
- 1 teaspoonoil
- 1 jalapeno pepper, chopped
- ½ cup lentils
- 3 cups chicken stock
- 1 teaspoon salt
- 1 tablespoon tomato paste
- 1 teaspoon chili pepper
- 3 tablespoons fresh cilantro, chopped
- 8 oz. cod, chopped.

**Directions:**

1. Placeoil, red pepper, onion, and ground black pepper in the saucepan.
2. Roast the vegetables for 5 minutes over the medium heat. Then add chopped jalapeno pepper, lentils, and chili pepper. Mix up the mixture well and add chicken stock and tomato paste.
3. Stir until homogenous. Add cod.
4. Close the lid and cook chili for 20 minutes over the medium heat.

**Nutrition:**
Calories: 187 Fat: 2.3g Fiber: 8.8g Carbs: 21.3g Protein: 20.6g.

## 70. SARDINE FISH CAKES
by Jan Cole – Sacramento

**Preparation Time:** 10 minutes
**Cooking Time:** 10 minutes

**Servings:** 4
**Ingredients:**

- 11 oz. sardines, canned, drained
- 1/3 cup shallot, chopped
- 1 teaspoon chili flakes
- ½ teaspoon salt
- 2 tablespoon wheat flour, whole grain
- 1 egg, beaten
- 1 tablespoon chives, chopped
- 1 teaspoon olive oil
- 1 teaspoon oil

**Directions:**

1. Put the oil in your skillet and dissolve it. Add shallot and cook it until translucent. After this, transfer the shallot to the mixing bowl.
2. Add sardines, chili flakes, salt, flour, egg, chives, and mix up until smooth with the fork's help. Make the medium size cakes and place them in the skillet. Add olive oil.
3. Roast the fish cakes for 3 minutes from each side over medium heat. Dry the cooked fish cakes with a paper towel if needed and transfer to the serving plates.

**Nutrition:**
Calories 221Fat 12.2g Fiber 0.1g Carbs 5.4g Protein 21.3 g Phosphorus 188.7 mg Potassium 160.3 mg Sodium 452.6 mg

## 71. 4-INGREDIENTS SALMON FILLET
by Henry Speed – Sugar Land

**Preparation Time:** 5 minutes
**Cooking Time:** 25 minutes
**Servings:** 1
**Ingredients:**

- 4 oz. salmon fillet
- ½ teaspoon salt
- 1 teaspoon sesame oil
- ½ teaspoon sage

**Directions:**

1. Rub the fillet with salt and sage. Put the fish in the tray, then sprinkle it with sesame oil. Cook the fish for 25 minutes at 365F. Flip the fish carefully onto another side after 12 minutes of cooking. Serve.

**Nutrition:**

Calories 191 Fat 11.6g Fiber 0.1g Carbs 0.2gP rotein 22g Sodium 70.5 mg Phosphorus 472 mg Potassium 636.3 mg

## 72. SPANISH COD IN SAUCE
by Betty Reeder – Baltimore

Preparation Time: 10 minutes
Cooking Time: 5 1/2 hours
Servings: 2

Ingredients:

- 1 teaspoon tomato paste
- 1 teaspoon garlic, diced
- 1 white onion, sliced
- 1 jalapeno pepper, chopped
- 1/3 cup chicken stock
- 7 oz. Spanish cod fillet
- 1 teaspoon paprika
- 1 teaspoon salt

Directions:

1. Pour chicken stock into the saucepan. Add tomato paste and mix up the liquid until homogenous. Add garlic, onion, jalapeno pepper, paprika, and salt.

2. Bring the liquid to boil and then simmer it. Chop the cod fillet and add it to the tomato liquid. Simmer the fish for 10 minutes over low heat. Serve the fish in the bowls with tomato sauce.

Nutrition:
Calories 113 Fat 1.2g Fiber 1.9g Carbs 7.2g Protein 18.9g Potassium 659 mg Sodium 597 mg Phosphorus 18 mg

## 73. SALMON BAKED IN FOIL WITH FRESH THYME
by Gloria Pate – Florence

Preparation Time: 10 minutes
Cooking Time: 30 minutes
Servings: 4

Ingredients:

- 4 fresh thyme sprigs
- 4 garlic cloves, peeled, roughly chopped
- 16 oz. salmon fillets (4 oz. each fillet)
- ½ teaspoon salt
- ½ teaspoon ground black pepper
- 4 tablespoons cream
- 4 teaspoons oil
- ¼ teaspoon cumin seeds

Directions:

1. Line the baking tray with foil. Sprinkle the fish fillets with salt, ground black pepper, cumin seeds, and arrange them in the tray with oil.

2. Add thyme sprig on the top of every fillet. Then add cream, oil, and garlic. Bake the fish for 30 minutes at 345F. Serve.

Nutrition:
Calories 198 Fat 11.6g Carbs 1.8g Protein 22.4g Phosphorus 425 mg Potassium 660.9 mg Sodium 366 mg

## 74. POACHED HALIBUT IN MANGO SAUCE
by Elias Rose – Carterville

Preparation Time: 10 minutes
Cooking Time: 10 minutes
Servings: 4

Ingredients:

- 1-pound halibut
- 1/3 cup oil
- 1 rosemary sprig
- ½ teaspoon ground black pepper
- 1 teaspoon salt
- 1 teaspoon honey
- ¼ cup of mango juice
- 1 teaspoon cornstarch

Directions:

1. Put oil in the saucepan and melt it. Add rosemary sprig. Sprinkle the halibut with salt and ground black pepper. Put the fish in the boiling oil and poach it for 4 minutes.

2. Meanwhile, pour mango juice into the skillet. Add honey and bring the liquid to boil. Add cornstarch and whisk until the liquid starts to be thick. Then remove it from the heat.

3. Transfer the poached halibut to the plate and cut it on 4. Place every fish serving in the serving plate and top with mango sauce.

Nutrition:

Calories 349 Fat 29.3g Fiber 0.1g  Carbs 3.2g Protein 17.8g
Phosphorus 154 mg Potassium 388.6 mg Sodium 29.3 mg

# CHAPTER 11
## WHITE MEAT

## 75. BAKED HERBED CHICKEN

**Preparation Time:** 10 minutes
**Cooking Time:** 60 minutes
**Servings:** 6
**Ingredients:**

- 1/4 tsp. pepper
- 6 chicken thighs, bone-in
- 1 tbsp. chopped oregano
- 1 tsp. lemon zest
- 1 tbsp. chopped parsley
- 4 garlic cloves, minced
- 4 tbsp.oil at room temperature

**Directions:**

1. Start by setting your oven to 425°F.
2. Add the lemon zest, parsley, oregano, garlic, andoil to a small bowl and mix well, making sure that everything is distributed evenly throughout theoil.
3. Lay the chicken on a baking pan and gently pull the skin back, but leaving it attached.
4. Brush the thigh meat with some of theoil mixture and lay the skin back over the meat. Sprinkle on some pepper.
5. Bake the chicken for 40 minutes. The skin should be crispy, and the juices should be clear. Also, the chicken should reach 165°F.
6. Allow the chicken to rest for 5 minutes before serving. Enjoy!

**Nutrition:**

Calories: 226 Protein: 16g Sodium: 120mg Potassium: 158mg Phosphorus: 114mg

## 76. CHICKEN AND CABBAGE STIR-FRY

**Preparation Time:** 5 minutes
**Cooking Time:** 8 minutes
**Servings:** 4
**Ingredients:**

- Pepper, to taste
- 1/4 cup water
- 1/2 tsp. garlic powder
- 1 tbsp. cornstarch
- 3 cups thinly sliced cabbage
- 1 tsp. ground ginger
- 10 oz. thinly sliced boneless, skinless chicken breast
- 1 tsp. canola oil

**Directions:**

1. Add the oil to a large skillet and heat. Add in the chicken and cook well, often stirring until it is cooked through and browned.
2. Add the cabbage into the skillet and cook for another 2 to 3 minutes. The cabbage should become tender, but it should still be green and crisp.
3. In a separate bowl, combine the water, garlic, ginger, and cornstarch. Pour this into the skillet and cook everything until the sauce has thickened up about 1 minute. Season with some pepper. Serve and enjoy!

**Nutrition:**

Calories: 96 Protein: 15g Sodium: 156mgPotassium: 140mg Phosphorus: 15mg

## 77. CHICKEN AND LEEK SALAD

**Preparation Time:** 15 minutes
**Cooking Time:** 30 minutes
**Servings:** 16
**Ingredients:**

- 450g chicken breast fillet
- Salt
- Pepper
- 2 tbsps. olive oil
- 3 bars leek
- 2 small apples (300g)
- ½ lemons (juice)
- 50ml of vegetable stock
- 2 tbsps. red wine vinegar
- 1 tsp. mustard
- 1 tsp. maple syrup
- 50g yogurt (3.5% fat)
- 1 tsp. paprika
- 1 tbsp. light sesame seeds (15g)

**Directions:**

1. Rinse chicken breast fillets, pat dry, and season with salt and pepper. Heat 1 tbsp. of oil in a pan; roast the chicken meat for 4–5 minutes, turning it over. Then place in an ovenproof dish and cook in a Preheated oven at 110°C

(circulating air 90°C, gas: stage 1–2) in about 8–10 minutes.

2. Meanwhile, fresh leek, wash and cut diagonally into rings, heat 1 tbsp. of oil in the pan. Brown leeks in medium heat for about 5 minutes, season with salt and pepper, remove from heat and let cool for 5 minutes. While doing so, wash apples, quarter them, core them, cut them into thin slices and drizzle with lemon juice.

3. Whisk the vegetable stock, vinegar, salt, pepper, mustard, maple syrup, and remaining oil and stir in the yogurt.

4. Take the roasted chicken from the oven and let it cool for 5 minutes. Mix the leek with the apple slices, spread on plates, and drizzle with the dressing. Slice chicken breasts in slices and place on plates. Sprinkle chicken and leek salad with paprika and sesame seeds and serve.

## Nutrition:

Calories: 290 Total Fat: 14g Cholesterol: 88mg Sodium: 82mg Potassium: 223mg Protein: 27g

## 78. CHICKEN CRANBERRY SAUCE SALAD

**Preparation Time:** 10 minutes
**Cooking Time:** 0 minutes
**Servings:** 6
**Ingredients:**

- 3 cups chicken meat, cooked, cubed
- 1 cup grapes
- 2 cups carrots, shredded
- 1/4 red onion, chopped
- 1 large yellow bell pepper, chopped
- 1/4 cup mayonnaise
- 1/2 cup cranberry sauce.

## Directions:

1. Put all the salad ingredients into a suitable salad bowl.
2. Toss them well and refrigerate for 1 hour.
3. Serve.

## Nutrition:

Calories: 240 Sodium: 161mg Carbohydrate: 19.4g Protein: 21g Calcium: 31mg Phosphorous: 260mg Potassium: 351mg.

## 79. CURRIED CHICKEN STIR-FRY

**Preparation Time:** 20 minutes
**Cooking Time:** 15 minutes

**Servings:** 6
**Ingredients:**

- 12 ounces chicken breasts, 1-inch cubes, boneless skinless
- 2 teaspoons curry powder
- 1/8 teaspoons salt
- 1/8 teaspoons freshly ground black pepper
- 1 (20-ounce) can pineapple tidbits, strained, reserving juice
- 2 tablespoons extra-virgin olive oil
- 1 yellow onion, chopped
- 2 red bell peppers, chopped

## Directions:

1. In a medium bowl, toss the chicken, curry powder, salt, and pepper and set aside.
2. In a small saucepan, heat the reserved pineapple juice over low heat. Let it reduce, occasionally stirring, while you make the rest of the stir-fry.
3. Heat the large skillet with olive oil in medium heat. Add the chicken. Stir-fry for 3 for 4 minutes or until the chicken is light brown; it doesn't have to completely cook. Transfer the chicken to a plate.
4. Put the onion to the skillet and cook for 3 minutes, stirring, until the onion is crisp-tender. Check to make sure the pineapple liquid isn't burning and continue to stir it. Add bell peppers then stir-fry it for another 3 minutes, until crisp-tender.
5. Put the chicken back to the skillet, add the pineapple tidbits and cook, stirring, for 3 to 4 minutes or until the chicken is cooked through.
6. Add the thickened pineapple juice to the skillet and stir. Serve.

## Nutrition:

Calories: 215 Total fat: 7g Saturated fat: 1g Sodium: 98mg Phosphorus: 146mg Potassium: 374mg Carbohydrates: 19g Fiber: 2g Protein: 19g Sugar: 16g

## 80. THAI-STYLE CHICKEN SALAD

**Preparation Time:** 10 minutes
**Cooking Time:** 20 minutes
**Servings:** 6
**Ingredients:**

- 3 cups (1 pound) cooked chicken, shredded

- 1 (10-ounce) package shredded cabbage with carrots
- 2 limes
- 1/3 cup extra-virgin olive oil
- ¼ cup peanutoil
- ¼ teaspoon freshly ground black pepper
- ¼ cup chopped peanuts.

## Directions:

1. Combine the chicken and cabbage and toss to mix in a large bowl.
2. In a small bowl, zest one of the limes. Juice both of the limes into the bowl. Add the olive oil, peanutoil, and pepper and mix with a whisk.
3. Drizzle the dressing over the salad and toss. Top with the peanuts and serve.

## Ingredient Tip:

If you like spicy food, add 1 or 2 minced jalapeño peppers to this salad. You could also add minced chipotle peppers in adobo sauce; just a teaspoon of each will add lots of heat.

## Nutrition:

Calories: 415 Total fat: 31g Saturated fat: 5g Sodium: 119mg Phosphorus: 239mg Potassium: 408mg Carbohydrates: 9g Fiber: 3g Protein: 28g Sugar: 3g

## 81. CREAMY CHICKEN

Preparation Time: 10 minutes
Cooking Time: 15 minutes
Servings: 2
Ingredients:

- 3 tbsp. oil
- 2 pounds cut into 1-inch thick strips skinless, boneless chicken breasts
- 4 minced garlic cloves
- ½ tsp. ground ginger
- ½ tsp. ground coriander
- ½ tsp. ground cumin
- ¼ tsp. crushed red pepper flakes
- ½ cup chicken broth
- 1/3 cup low-fat sour cream
- 1 tbsp. chopped fresh parsley

## Directions:

1. In a large skillet, meltoil on medium-high heat.

2. Add chicken and cook for about 5–6 minutes.
3. Add garlic and spices and cook for 1 minute.
4. Add broth and bring to a boil. Reduce the heat to medium-low.
5. Simmer for about 5 minutes, stirring occasionally.
6. Stir in cream and simmer, occasionally stirring for about 3 minutes.
7. Serve hot with the garnishing of parsley.

## Nutrition:

Calories: 206 Fat: 10.5g Carbs: 1.2gProtein: 26.1g Fiber: 0g Potassium: 43mgSodium: 144mg

## 82. FABULOUS CHICKEN

Preparation Time: 10 minutes
Cooking Time: 15 minutes
Servings: 8
Ingredients:

- 1 cup low-sodium chicken broth
- 3 tbsp. balsamic vinegar
- 2 tsp. cornstarch
- 2 tbsp. olive oil
- 4 minced garlic cloves
- 2 tbsp. minced fresh basil
- 4 (4-ounce) skinless, boneless chicken breasts
- Pinch salt
- Freshly ground black pepper, to taste

## Directions:

1. In a bowl, mix broth, vinegar, and cornstarch.
2. In a large skillet, heat oil on medium-high heat.
3. Add garlic and basil and sauté for about 1 minute.
4. Add chicken and sprinkle with salt and black pepper.
5. Cook for about 12–15 minutes. Transfer the chicken into a bowl.
6. Add broth mixture and bring to a boil, cook for about 1 minute.
7. Reduce the heat to low.
8. Stir in chicken and cook for about 3–4 minutes.

## Nutrition:

Calories: 279 Fat: 11.2gCarbs: 18.8g Protein: 26.4gFiber: 3.8g Potassium: 145mgSodium: 60mg

## 83.  DIVINE GROUND CHICKEN

**Preparation Time:** 10minutes
**Cooking Time:** 21 minutes
**Servings:** 5
**Ingredients:**

- 1¼ pound lean ground chicken
- 1 small sliced onion
- 2 tsp. minced garlic
- 1 tsp. ground cumin
- 1 tsp. ground coriander
- 1/8 tsp. ground turmeric
- 1/8 tsp. cayenne pepper
- Pinch salt
- Freshly ground black pepper
- 1 chopped medium tomato
- 1 cup water
- ¼ cup chopped fresh cilantro, chopped

**Directions:**

1. Heat a nonstick skillet on medium-high heat.
2. Add chicken, onion and garlic and cook for about 5–6 minutes or till browned.
3. Remove any excess fat from the skillet.
4. Add spices and tomato cook for about 2 minutes.
5. Stir in water and bring to a gentle boil.
6. Reduce the heat to medium-low and simmer, covered for about 10–15 minutes.
7. Stir in cilantro and serve immediately.

**Nutrition:**

Calories: 164 Fat: 6.2gCarbs: 2.9gProtein: 23.5gFiber: 0.7gPotassium: 161mgSodium: 99mg

## 84.  COMFORTING CHICKEN CHILI

**Preparation Time:** 10 minutes
**Cooking Time:** 2 hours
**Servings:** 12
**Ingredients:**

- 2 tbsp. olive oil
- 1 chopped large onion
- 1 seeded and chopped medium green bell pepper
- 1 seeded and chopped medium red bell pepper
- 4 minced garlic cloves
- 1 chopped jalapeño pepper
- 1 tsp. crushed dried basil
- 1 tsp. crushed dried thyme
- 1 tbsp. red chili powder
- 1 tbsp. ground cumin
- 2 pound lean ground chicken
- 8-ounce low-sodium tomato paste
- 2 cups low-sodium chicken broth
- 2 cups water

**Directions:**

1. In a large pan, heat oil on medium heat.
2. Add onion and bell pepper and sauté for about 5–7 minutes.
3. Add garlic, jalapeño pepper, herbs, spices, and black pepper and sauté for about 1 minute.
4. Add chicken and cook for about 4–5 minutes.
5. Stir in tomato paste and cook for about 2 minutes.
6. Add broth and water and bring to a boil.
7. Reduce the heat to low and simmer, covered for about 1-1½ hours or till the desired doneness.
8. Serve hot.

**Nutrition:**

Calories: 155 Fat: 6.7gCarbs: 7.4g Protein: 17.1gFiber: 1.6g Potassium: 275mg Sodium: 123mg

## 85.  CARIBBEAN TURKEY CURRY

**Preparation Time:** 10 minutes
**Cooking Time:** 1 hour 30 minutes
**Servings:** 6
**Ingredients:**

- 3 1/2 lbs. turkey breast, with skin
- 1/4 cupoil, melted
- 1/4 cup honey
- 1 tbsp. mustard
- 2 tsp. curry powder
- 1 tsp. garlic powder

**Directions:**

1. Place the turkey breast in a shallow roasting pan.
2. Insert a meat thermometer to monitor the temperature.

3. Bake the turkey for 1.5 hours at 350°F until its internal temperature reaches 170°F.
4. Meanwhile, thoroughly mix honey, oil, curry powder, garlic powder, and mustard in a bowl.
5. Glaze the cooked turkey with this mixture liberally.
6. Let it sit for 15 minutes for absorption.
7. Slice and serve.

## Nutrition:

Calories: 275Protein: 26gCarbohydrates: 9gFat: 13gCholesterol: 82mgSodium: 122mgPotassium: 277mgPhosphorus: 193mgCalcium: 24mgFiber: 0.2g

## 86. CHICKEN STEW

**Preparation Time:** 20 minutes
**Cooking Time:** 50 minutes
**Servings:** 6
**Ingredients:**

- 1 tbsp. olive oil
- 1 pound chicken thighs - boneless, skinless (1-inch cubes)
- ½ sweet onion, chopped
- 1 tbsp. minced garlic
- 2 cups chicken stock
- 1 cup, plus 2 tbsp. water
- 1 sliced carrot
- 2 stalks celery, sliced
- 1 turnip, sliced thin
- 1 tbsp. chopped fresh thyme
- 1 tsp. chopped fresh rosemary
- 2 tsp. cornstarch
- Ground black pepper to taste.

**Directions:**

1. Place a large saucepan on medium heat and add the olive oil.
2. Sauté the chicken for 6 minutes or until it is lightly browned, stirring often.
3. Add the onion and garlic, and sauté for 3 minutes.
4. Add 1 cup of water, chicken stock, carrot, celery, and turnip and bring the stew to a boil.
5. Reduce the heat to low and simmer for 30 minutes or until the chicken is cooked through and tender.

6. Add the thyme and rosemary and simmer for 3 minutes more.
7. In a small bowl, stir together the 2 tbsp. of water and the cornstarch
8. Add the mixture to the stew.
9. Stir to incorporate the cornstarch mixture and cook for 3 to 4 minutes or until the stew thickens.
10. Remove from the heat and season with pepper.

## Nutrition:

Calories: 141 Fat: 8g Carb: 5g Phosphorus: 53mgPotassium: 192mg Sodium: 214mg Protein: 9g

## 87. ASIAN STYLE PAN-FRIED CHICKEN

**Preparation Time:** 10 minutes
**Cooking Time:** 20 minutes
**Servings:** 4
**Ingredients:**

- 1 lemon, cut into wedges
- 3 tsp. canola oil, divided
- 1/2 cup cornstarch
- 1 tsp. low sodium soy sauce
- 1-inch piece minced ginger
- 1 tsp. dry rice wine
- 12 oz. chicken thighs, boneless and skinless

**Directions:**

1. Mix the soy sauce, ginger, rice wine, and chicken.
2. Toss everything together and allow it to marinate for 15 minutes.
3. Toss the chicken one more time and then drain off the liquid. One at a time, dip the chicken pieces into the cornstarch so that they are coated.
4. Heat 1.5 teaspoons of oil on medium-high in a medium skillet.
5. Add in half of the chicken to the skillet and cook until it has turned golden brown on one side, around 3 to 5 minutes. Turn the chicken over and continue to cook until the chicken has cooked through and browned. Place on a plate lined with a paper towel to cool and to absorb excess oil.
6. Add in the remaining oil and cook the rest of the chicken thighs.
7. Serve the chicken with a garnish of lemon. Enjoy!

## Nutrition:

Calories: 198 Protein: 17gSodium: 119mg Potassium: 218mg Phosphorus: 148mg

## 88. CURRIED CHICKEN WITH CAULIFLOWER

**Preparation Time:** 20 minutes
**Cooking Time:** 2 hours and 30 minutes
**Servings:** 6
**Ingredients:**

- Lime juice 2 limes
- 1/2 tsp. dried oregano
- Cauliflower head, cut into florets
- 4 tsp. EVOO, divided
- 6 chicken thighs, bone-in
- 1/2 tsp. pepper, divided
- 1/4 tsp. paprika
- 1/2 tsp. ground cumin
- 3 tbsp. curry powder

**Directions:**

1. Mix a quarter of a tsp. of pepper, paprika, cumin, and curry in a small bowl.
2. Add the chicken thighs to a medium bowl and drizzle with 2 tsp. of olive oil and sprinkle in the curry mixture.
3. Toss them together so that the chicken is well coated.
4. Cover this up and refrigerate it for at least 2 hours.
5. Now set your oven to 400°F.
6. Toss the cauliflower, remaining oil, and the oregano together in a medium bowl. Arrange the cauliflower and chicken across a baking sheet in one layer.
7. Allow this to bake for 40 minutes. Stir the cauliflower and flip the chicken once during the cooking time. The chicken should be browned, and the juices should run clear. The temperature of the chicken should reach 165°F.
8. Serve with some lime juice. Enjoy!

**Nutrition:**

Calories: 175 Protein: 16g Sodium: 77mg Potassium: 486mg Phosphorus: 152mg

## 89. RED AND GREEN GRAPES CHICKEN SALAD WITH CURRY

**Preparation Time:** 5 minutes
**Cooking Time:** 0 minute
**Servings:** 2

**Ingredients:**

- 1 apple
- 1/4 bowl seedless, red grapes
- 1/4 bowl seedless, green grapes
- 4 cooked skinless and boneless chicken breasts
- 1 piece celery
- 1/2 bowl onion
- 1/2 bowl canned water chestnuts
- 1/2 tsp. curry powder
- 3/4 cup mayonnaise
- 1/8 tsp. black pepper

**Directions:**

1. Cut the chicken into small dices and chop celery, onion, and apple. Drain and cut chestnuts.
2. Put together the chicken pieces, celery, onion, apple, grapes, water chestnuts, pepper, curry powder, and mayonnaise.
3. Serve it in a big salad bowl. Enjoy!

**Nutrition:**

Calories: 235 Protein: 13g Sodium: 160mg Potassium: 200mg Phosphrus: 115mg

## 90. GRILLED CHICKEN PIZZA

**Preparation Time:** 20 minutes
**Cooking Time:** 15 minutes
**Servings:** 2
**Ingredients:**

- 2 pita bread
- 3 tbsp. low sodium BBQ sauce
- 1/4 bowl red onion
- 4 oz. cooked chicken
- 2 tbsp. crumbled feta cheese
- 1/8 tsp. garlic powder

**Directions:**

1. Preheat oven at 350°F (that is 175°C).
2. Place 2 pitas on the pan after you have put non-stick cooking spray on it.
3. Spread BBQ sauce (2 tablespoons) on the pita.
4. Cut the onion and put it on pita. Cube chicken and put it on the pitas.
5. Put also both feta and the garlic powder over the pita.

6. Bake for 12 minutes. Serve and enjoy!

## Nutrition:

Calories: 320  Protein: 22g  Sodium: 520mg  Potassium: 250mg  Phosphorus: 220mg

## 91. CHICKEN BREAST AND BOK CHOY

Preparation Time: 10 minutes
Cooking Time: 30 minutes
Servings: 4
Ingredients:

- 4 slices lemon
- Pepper, to taste
- 4 chicken breasts, boneless and skinless
- 1 tbsp. Dijon mustard
- 1 small leek, thinly sliced
- 2 julienned carrots
- 2 cups thinly sliced book choy
- 1 tbsp. chopped thyme
- 1 tbsp. EVOO

## Directions:

1. Start by setting your oven to 425°F.
2. Mix the thyme, olive oil, and mustard in a small bowl.
3. Take four 18-inch-long pieces of parchment paper and fold them in half. Cut them like you would make a heart. Open each of the pieces and lay them flat.
4. In each parchment piece, place .5 cup of book choy, a few slices of leek, and a small handful of carrots.
5. Lay the chicken breast on top and season with some pepper.
6. Brush the chicken breasts with the marinade and top each one with a slice of lemon.
7. Fold the packets up, and roll down the edges to seal the packages.
8. Allow them to cook for 20 minutes. Let them rest of 5 minutes, and make sure you open them carefully when serving. Enjoy!

## Nutrition:

Calories: 164  Protein: 24g Sodium: 356mg  Potassium: 189mg  Phosphorus: 26mg  Phosphorus: 26mg

## 92. GRILLED CHICKEN WITH PINEAPPLE & VEGGIES

Preparation Time: 20 or so minutes
Cooking Time: 22 minutes
Servings: 4
Ingredients:

- For Sauce:
- 1 garlic oil, minced
- ¾ teaspoon fresh ginger, minced
- ½ cup coconut aminos
- ¼ cup fresh pineapple juice
- 2 tablespoons freshly squeezed lemon juice
- 2 tablespoons balsamic vinegar
- ¼ teaspoon red pepper flakes, crushed
- Salt
- ground black pepper
- For Grilling:
- 4 skinless, boneless chicken breasts
- 1 pineapple, peeled and sliced
- 1 bell pepper, seeded and cubed
- 1 zucchini, sliced
- 1 red onion, sliced

## Directions:

1. For sauce in a pan, mix all ingredients on medium-high heat. Bring to a boil reducing the heat to medium-low. Cook approximately 5-6 minutes.
2. Remove, then keep aside to cool down slightly. Coat the chicken breasts about ¼ from the sauce. Keep aside for approximately half an hour.
3. Preheat the grill to medium-high heat. Grease the grill grate. Grill the chicken pieces for around 5-8 minutes per side.
4. Now, squeeze pineapple and vegetables on the grill grate. Grill the pineapple within 3 minutes per side. Grill the vegetables for approximately 4-5 minutes, stirring once inside the middle way.
5. Cut the chicken breasts into desired size slices, divide the chicken, pineapple, and vegetables into serving plates. Serve alongside the remaining sauce.

## Nutrition:

Calories: 435  Fat: 12g  Carbohydrates: 25g  Protein: 38g  Phosphorus 184 mg  Potassium 334.4 mg  Sodium 755.6 mg

## 93. GROUND TURKEY WITH VEGGIES

**Preparation Time:** 15 minutes
**Cooking Time:** 12 minutes
**Servings:** 4
**Ingredients:**

- 1 tablespoon sesame oil
- 1 tablespoon coconut oil
- 1-pound lean ground turkey
- 2 tablespoons fresh ginger, minced
- 2 minced garlic cloves
- 1 (16-ounce) bag vegetable mix (broccoli, carrot, cabbage, kale, and Brussels sprouts)
- ¼ cup coconut aminos
- 2 tablespoons balsamic vinegar

### Directions:

1. In a big skillet, heat both oils on medium-high heat. Add turkey, ginger, and garlic and cook approximately 5-6 minutes. Add vegetable mix and cook about 4-5 minutes. Stir in coconut aminos and vinegar and cook for about 1 minute. Serve hot.

### Nutrition:

Calories: 234 Fat: 9g Carbohydrates: 9g Protein: 29g Phosphorus 14 mg Potassium 92.2 mg Sodium 114.9 mg

## 94. GROUND TURKEY WITH ASPARAGUS

**Preparation Time:** 15 minutes
**Cooking Time:** 15 minutes
**Servings:** 8
**Ingredients:**

- 1¾ pound lean ground turkey
- 2 tablespoons sesame oil
- 1 medium onion, chopped
- 1 cup celery, chopped
- 6 garlic cloves, minced
- 2 cups asparagus, cut into 1-inch pieces
- 1/3 cup coconut aminos
- 2½ teaspoons ginger powder
- 2 tablespoons organic coconut crystals
- 1 tablespoon arrowroot starch
- 1 tablespoon cold water

- ¼ teaspoon red pepper flakes, crushed

### Directions:

1. Heat a substantial nonstick skillet on medium-high heat. Add turkey and cook for approximately 5-7 minutes or till browned. With a slotted spoon, transfer the turkey inside a bowl and discard the grease from the skillet.

2. Heat-up oil on medium heat in the same skillet. Add onion, celery, and garlic and sauté for about 5 minutes. Add asparagus and cooked turkey, minimizing the temperature to medium-low.

3. Meanwhile, inside a pan, mix coconut aminos, ginger powder, and coconut crystals n medium heat and convey some boil.

4. Mix arrowroot starch and water in a smaller bowl. Slowly add arrowroot mixture, stirring continuously. Cook approximately 2-3 minutes.

5. Add the sauce in the skillet with turkey mixture and stir to blend. Stir in red pepper flakes and cook for approximately 2-3 minutes. Serve hot.

### Nutrition:

Calories: 309 Fat: 20g Carbohydrates: 19g Protein: 28g Potassium 196.4 mg Sodium 77.8 mg Phosphorus 0 mg

## 95. GROUND TURKEY WITH PEAS & POTATO
by Gregory Shaw – York

**Preparation Time:** 15 minutes
**Cooking Time:** 35 minutes
**Servings:** 4
**Ingredients:**

- 3-4 tablespoons coconut oil
- 1-pound lean ground turkey
- 1-2 fresh red chilis, chopped
- 1 onion, chopped
- Salt, to taste
- 2 minced garlic cloves
- 1 (1-inch) piece fresh ginger, grated finely
- 1 tablespoon curry powder
- 1 teaspoon ground coriander
- 1 teaspoon ground cumin
- 1 teaspoon ground turmeric
- 2 large Yukon gold carrots, cubed into 1-inch size
- ½ cup of water

- 1 cup fresh peas, shelled
- 2-4 plum Red bell peppers, chopped
- ½ cup fresh cilantro, chopped

## Directions:

1. In a substantial pan, heat oil on medium-high heat. Add turkey and cook for about 4-5 minutes. Add chilis and onion and cook for about 4-5 minutes.

2. Add garlic and ginger and cook approximately 1-2 minutes. Stir in spices, carrots, and water and convey to your boil

3. Reduce the warmth to medium-low. Simmer covered around 15-20 or so minutes. Add peas and Red bell peppers and cook for about 2-3 minutes. Serve using the garnishing of cilantro.

## Nutrition:

Calories: 452 Fat: 14g Carbohydrates: 24g Fiber: 13g Protein: 36g Phosphorus 38 mg Potassium 99.5 mg Sodium 373.4 mg

## 96. ROASTED SPATCHCOCK CHICKEN
by Richard Miller – Winter Park

Preparation Time: 20 minutes
Cooking Time: 50 minutes
Servings: 4-6

## Ingredients:

- 1 (4-pound) whole chicken
- 1 (1-inch) piece fresh ginger, sliced
- 4 garlic cloves, chopped
- 1 small bunch of fresh thyme
- Pinch of cayenne
- Salt
- ground black pepper
- ¼ cup fresh lemon juice
- 3 tablespoons extra virgin olive oil

## Directions:

1. Arrange chicken, breast side down onto a large cutting board. With a kitchen shear, begin with the thigh, cut along 1 side of the backbone, and turn the chicken around.

2. Now, cut along sleep issues and discard the backbone. Change the inside and open it like a book. Flatten the backbone firmly to flatten.

3. In a food processor, add all ingredients except chicken and pulse till smooth. In a big baking dish, add the marinade mixture.

4. Add chicken and coat with marinade generously. With a plastic wrap, cover the baking dish and refrigerate to marinate overnight.

5. Preheat the oven to 450 degrees F. Arrange a rack in a very roasting pan. Remove the chicken from the refrigerator makes onto a rack over the roasting pan, skin side down. Roast for about 50 minutes, turning once in a middle way.

## Nutrition:

Calories: 419 Fat: 14g Carbohydrates: 28g Protein: 40g Phosphorus 166 mg Potassium 196 mg Sodium 68 mg

## 97. ROASTED CHICKEN WITH VEGGIES & MANGO
by Shannon Renteria – Chicago

Preparation Time: 20 minutes
Cooking Time: 1 hour
Servings: 4

## Ingredients:

- 1 teaspoon ground ginger
- ½ teaspoon ground cumin
- ½ teaspoon ground coriander
- 1 teaspoon paprika
- Salt
- ground black pepper
- 1 (3 ½-4-pound) whole chicken
- 1 unpeeled mango, cut into 8 wedges
- 2 medium carrots, peeled and cut 1nto 2-inch pieces
- ½ cup of water

## Directions:

1. Warm oven to 450 degrees F. In a little bowl, mix the spices. Rub the chicken with spice mixture evenly.

2. Arrange the chicken in a substantial Dutch oven and put the mango, carrot, and sweet potato pieces around it.

3. Add water and cover the pan tightly. Roast for around 30 minutes. Uncover and roast for about half an hour.

## Nutrition:

Calories: 432 Fat: 10g Carbohydrates: 20g Protein: 34g Potassium 481 mg Sodium 418 mg Phosphorus 170 mg

## 98. ROASTED CHICKEN BREAST
by Tina Dungan – Hartford

**Preparation Time:** 15 minutes
**Cooking Time:** 40 minutes
**Servings:** 4-6

### Ingredients:

- ½ of a small apple, peeled, cored, and chopped
- 1 bunch scallion, trimmed and chopped roughly
- 8 fresh ginger slices, chopped
- 2 garlic cloves, chopped
- 3 tablespoons essential olive oil
- 12 teaspoon sesame oil, toasted
- 3 tablespoons using apple cider vinegar
- 1 tablespoon fish sauce
- 1 tablespoon coconut aminos
- Salt
- ground black pepper
- 4-pounds chicken thighs

### Directions:

1. Pulse all the fixing except chicken thighs in a blender. Transfer a combination and chicken right into a large Ziploc bag and seal it.
2. Shake the bag to marinade well. Refrigerate to marinate for about 12 hours. Warm oven to 400 degrees F. arranges a rack in foil paper-lined baking sheet.
3. Place the chicken thighs on the rack, skin-side down. Roast for about 40 minutes, flipping once within the middle way.

### Nutrition:
Calories: 451 Fat: 17g Carbohydrates: 277g Protein: 42g Phosphorus 121 mg Potassium 324 mg Sodium 482.9 mg

## 99. GRILLED CHICKEN
by Jesus Bingham – Charlotte

**Preparation Time:** 15 minutes
**Cooking Time:** 41 minutes
**Servings:** 8

### Ingredients:

- 1 (3-inch) piece fresh ginger, minced
- 6 small garlic cloves, minced

- 1½ tablespoons tamarind paste
- 1 tablespoon organic honey
- ¼ cup coconut aminos
- 2½ tablespoons extra virgin olive oil
- 1½ tablespoons sesame oil, toasted
- ½ teaspoon ground cardamom
- Salt
- ground white pepper
- 1 (4-5-pound) whole chicken, cut into 8 pieces

### Directions:

1. Mix all ingredients except chicken pieces in a large glass bowl. With a fork, pierce the chicken pieces thoroughly.
2. Add chicken pieces in bowl and coat with marinade generously. Cover and refrigerate to marinate for approximately a couple of hours to overnight.
3. Preheat the grill to medium heat. Grease the grill grate. Place the chicken pieces on the grill, bone-side down. Grill, covered approximately 20-25 minutes.
4. Change the side and grill, covered approximately 6-8 minutes. Change alongside it and grill, covered for about 5-8 minutes. Serve.

### Nutrition:
Calories: 423 Fat: 12g Carbohydrates: 20g Protein: 42g Sodium 281.9 mg Phosphorus 0 mg Potassium 0 mg

## 100. GROUND CHICKEN WITH BASIL
by Earline Pafford – Fort Myers

**Preparation Time:** 15 minutes
**Cooking Time:** 16 minutes
**Servings:** 8

### Ingredients:

- 2 pounds lean ground chicken
- 3 tablespoons coconut oil, divided
- 1 zucchini, chopped
- 1 red bell pepper, seeded and chopped
- ½ of green bell pepper, seeded and chopped
- 4 garlic cloves, minced
- 1 (1-inch) piece fresh ginger, minced
- 1 (1-inch) piece fresh turmeric, minced
- 1 fresh red chili, sliced thinly
- 1 tablespoon organic honey

- 1 tablespoon coconut aminos
- 1½ tablespoons fish sauce
- ½ cup fresh basil, chopped
- Salt
- ground black pepper
- 1 tablespoon fresh lime juice

## Directions:

1. Heat a large skillet on medium-high heat. Add ground beef and cook for approximately 5 minutes or till browned completely.

2. Transfer the beef to a bowl. In a similar pan, melt 1 tablespoon of coconut oil on medium-high heat. Add zucchini and bell peppers and stir fry for around 3-4 minutes.

3. Transfer the vegetables inside the bowl with chicken. In precisely the same pan, melt remaining coconut oil on medium heat. Add garlic, ginger, turmeric, and red chili and sauté for approximately 1-2 minutes.

4. Add chicken mixture, honey, and coconut aminos and increase the heat to high. Cook within 4-5 minutes or till sauce is nearly reduced. Stir in remaining ingredients and take off from the heat.

## Nutrition:

Calories: 407 Fat: 7g Carbohydrates: 20g Fiber: 13g Protein: 36g Phosphorus 149 mg Potassium 706.3 mg    Sodium 21.3 mg

---

## 101. CHICKEN &VEGGIE CASSEROLE
by ESidney Frazier – Groton

**Preparation Time:** 15 minutes
**Cooking Time:** 30 minutes
**Servings:** 4

### Ingredients:

- 1/3 cup Dijon mustard
- 1/3 cup organic honey
- 1 teaspoon dried basil
- ¼ teaspoon ground turmeric
- 1 teaspoon dried basil, crushed
- Salt
- ground black pepper
- 1¾ pound chicken breasts
- 1 cup fresh white mushrooms, sliced
- ½ head broccoli, cut into small florets

## Directions:

1. Warm oven to 350 degrees F. Lightly greases a baking dish. In a bowl, mix all ingredients except chicken, mushrooms, and broccoli.

2. Put the chicken in your prepared baking dish, then top with mushroom slices. Place broccoli florets around chicken evenly.

3. Pour 1 / 2 of honey mixture over chicken and broccoli evenly. Bake for approximately 20 minutes. Now, coat the chicken with the remaining sauce and bake for about 10 minutes.

## Nutrition:

Calories: 427 Fat: 9g Carbohydrates: 16g Fiber: 7g Protein: 35g Phosphorus 353 mg Potassium 529.3 mg Sodium 1 mg

---

## 102. CHICKEN & CAULIFLOWER RICE CASSEROLE
by Sandra Machado – Poseyville

**Preparation Time:** 15 minutes
**Cooking Time:** 1 hour & 15 minutes
**Servings:** 8-10

### Ingredients:

- 2 tablespoons coconut oil, divided
- 3-pound bone-in chicken thighs and drumsticks
- Salt
- ground black pepper
- 3 carrots, peeled and sliced
- 1 onion, chopped finely
- 2 garlic cloves, chopped finely
- 2 tablespoons fresh cinnamon, chopped finely
- 2 teaspoons ground cumin
- 1 teaspoon ground coriander
- 12 teaspoon ground cinnamon
- ½ teaspoon ground turmeric
- 1 teaspoon paprika
- ¼ tsp red pepper cayenne
- 1 (28-ounce) can diced Red bell peppers with liquid
- 1 red bell pepper, thin strips
- ½ cup fresh parsley leaves, minced
- Salt, to taste
- 1 head cauliflower, grated to some rice-like consistency

- 1 lemon, sliced thinly

## Directions:

1. Warm oven to 375 degrees F. In a large pan, melt 1 tablespoon of coconut oil at high heat. Add chicken pieces and cook for about 3-5 minutes per side or till golden brown.

2. Transfer the chicken to a plate. In a similar pan, sauté the carrot, onion, garlic, and ginger for about 4-5 minutes on medium heat.

3. Stir in spices and remaining coconut oil. Add chicken, Red bell peppers, bell pepper, parsley plus salt, and simmer for approximately 3-5 minutes.

4. In the bottom of a 13x9-inch rectangular baking dish, spread the cauliflower rice evenly. Place chicken mixture over cauliflower rice evenly and top with lemon slices.

5. With foil paper, cover the baking dish and bake for approximately 35 minutes. Uncover the baking dish and bake for about 25 minutes.

### Nutrition:
Calories: 412 Fat: 12g Carbohydrates: 23g Protein: 34g Phosphorus 201 mg Potassium 289.4 mg Sodium 507.4 mg

## 103. CHICKEN MEATLOAF WITH VEGGIES
by Blanca Hurt – Corpus Christi

**Preparation Time:** 20 minutes
**Cooking Time:** 1-1¼ hours
**Servings:** 4

### Ingredients:

- For Meatloaf:
- ½ cup cooked chickpeas
- 2 egg whites
- 2½ teaspoons poultry seasoning
- Salt
- ground black pepper
- 10-ounce lean ground chicken
- 1 cup red bell pepper, seeded and minced
- 1 cup celery stalk, minced
- 1/3 cup steel-cut oats
- 1 cup tomato puree, divided
- 2 tablespoons dried onion flakes, crushed
- 1 tablespoon prepared mustard
- For Veggies:

- 2-pounds summer squash, sliced
- 16-ounce frozen Brussels sprouts
- 2 tablespoons extra-virgin extra virgin olive oil
- Salt
- ground black pepper

## Directions:

1. Warm oven to 350 degrees F. Grease a 9x5-inch loaf pan. In a mixer, add chickpeas, egg whites, poultry seasoning, salt, and black pepper and pulse till smooth.

2. Transfer a combination in a large bowl. Add chicken, veggies oats, ½ cup of tomato puree, and onion flakes and mix till well combined.

3. Transfer the amalgamation into the prepared loaf pan evenly. With both hands, press down the amalgamation slightly.

4. In another bowl, mix mustard and remaining tomato puree. Place the mustard mixture over the loaf pan evenly.

5. Bake approximately 1-1¼ hours or till the desired doneness. Meanwhile, in a big pan of water, arrange a steamer basket. Cover and steam for about 10-12 minutes. Drain well and aside.

6. Now, prepare the Brussels sprouts according to the package's directions. In a big bowl, add veggies, oil, salt, and black pepper and toss to coat well. Serve the meatloaf with veggies.

### Nutrition:
Calories: 420 Fat: 9g Carbohydrates: 21g Protein: 36g Phosphorus 237.1 mg Potassium 583.6 mg Sodium 136

# CHAPTER 12

# VEGETARIAN RECIPES AND VEGANS

BE PART OF THIS COMMUNITY OF CRAZY INNOVATORS AND SHARE
YOUR UNCONVENTIONAL KNOWLEDGE...BE PART OF ...
FUN CLUB KITCHEN

## 104. MIXED PEPPER PAELLA

**Preparation Time:** 10 minutes
**Cooking Time:** 35-40 minutes
**Servings:** 2
**Ingredients:**

- 1 tbsp. extra virgin olive oil
- ½ chopped red onion
- 1 lemon
- ½ chopped yellow bell pepper
- 1 cup homemade chicken broth
- ½ chopped zucchini
- 1 tsp. dried oregano
- ½ chopped red bell pepper
- 1 tsp. dried parsley
- 1 cup brown rice
- 1 tsp. paprika

**Directions:**

1. Add the rice to a pot of cold water and cook for 15 minutes.
2. Drain the water, cover the pan and leave to one side.
3. Heat the oil in a skillet over medium-high heat.
4. Add the bell peppers, onion and zucchini, sautéing for 5 minutes.
5. To the pan, add the rice, herbs, spices and juice of the lemon along with the chicken broth.
6. Cover and turn the heat right down and allow to simmer for 15-20 minutes.
7. Serve hot.

**Nutrition:**

Calories 210 Protein 4 g Carbs 33 gFat 7 g Sodium (Na) 20 mg Potassium (K) 33 mg Phosphorus 156 mg

## 105. CAULIFLOWER RICE & RUNNY EGGS

**Preparation Time:** 5 minutes
**Cooking Time:** 30 minutes
**Servings:** 4
**Ingredients:**

- 4 eggs
- 1 tbsp. extra virgin olive oil
- 1 tsp. black pepper
- 1 tbsp. chopped fresh chives
- 2 cups cauliflower
- 1 tbsp. curry powder

**Directions:**

1. Preheat the oven to 375°F/Gas Mark 5.
2. Soak the cauliflower in warm water in advance if possible.
3. Grate or chop into rice-size pieces.
4. Bring the cauliflower to the boil in a pot of water and then turn down to simmer for 7 minutes.
5. Drain completely.
6. Place on a baking tray and sprinkle over curry powder and black pepper - toss to coat.
7. Bake in the oven for 20 minutes, stirring occasionally.
8. Meanwhile, boil a separate pan of water and add the eggs for 7 minutes.
9. Run under the cold tap, crack and peel the eggs before cutting in half.
10. Top the cauliflower with eggs and chopped chives.
11. Serve hot!

**Nutrition:**

Calories 120Protein 7 g Carbs 4 gFat 8 g Sodium (Na) 175 mg Potassium (K) 188 mg Phosphorus 134 mg

## 106. MINTED ZUCCHINI NOODLES

**Preparation Time:**5 minutes
**Cooking Time:** 10 minutes
**Servings:** 2
**Ingredients:**

- ¼ deseeded and chopped red chili
- 2 tbsps. Extra virgin olive oil
- ½ juiced lemon
- 4 peeled and sliced zucchinis
- ½ cup chopped fresh mint
- 1 tsp. black pepper
- ½ cup arugula

**Directions:**

1. Whisk the mint, pepper, chili and olive oil to make a dressing.
2. Meanwhile, heat a pan of water on a high heat and bring to the boil.
3. Add the zucchini noodles and turn the heat down to simmer for 3-4 minutes.

4. Remove from the heat and place in a bowl of cold water immediately.
5. Toss the noodles in the dressing.
6. Mix the arugula with the lemon juice to serve on the top.
7. Enjoy!

## Nutrition:

Calories 148 Protein 2 Carbs 4 g, Fat 13 g, Sodium (Na) 7 mgPotassium (K) 422 mPhosphorus 256 mg

## 107. LENTIL VEGAN SOUP

**Preparation Time:** 10 minutes
**Cooking Time:** 50 minutes
**Servings:** 5
**Ingredients:**

- Olive oil - 2 tablespoons
- Onion (diced) - 1
- Garlic (minced) - 2 cloves
- Carrot (diced) - 1
- Potatoes (diced) - 2
- Tomato (diced) - 1 can (15 ounces)
- Dried lentil - 2 cups
- Vegetable broth - 8 cups
- Bay leaf - 1
- Cumin - ½ teaspoon
- Salt – as per taste
- Pepper – as per taste

## Directions:

1. Start by taking a large pot and add in 2 tablespoons of olive oil. Place the pot over medium flame.
2. Once the oil heats through, toss in the onions and cook for 5 minutes.
3. Add in the garlic and cook for another 2 minutes.
4. Now toss in the diced potatoes and carrots. Sauté for about 3 minutes.
5. Add the remaining ingredients like vegetable broth, tomatoes, lentils, cumin and bay leaf.
6. Once it comes to a boil, reduce the flame to low and cook for about 40 minutes.
7. Remove the bay leaf and season with pepper and salt.
8. Transfer into a serving bowl. Serve hot!

## Nutrition:

Calories: 364 calories Fat – 7 g Carbohydrates – 58 g Protein – 19 g

## 108. CHICKPEA AND AVOCADO SALAD

**Preparation Time:** 15 minutes
**Cooking Time:** 0 minutes
**Servings:** 4
**Ingredients:**
**Dressing:**

- Olive oil - 2 tablespoons
- Lime juice - ¼ cup
- Cumin - 2 teaspoons
- Chili powder - 2 teaspoons
- Salt - 1 teaspoon
- Pepper - 1 teaspoon
- Fresh cilantro (chopped) - ¼ cup

## Salad:

- Chickpeas (rinsed and drained) - 2 cans
- Cucumber (quartered and chopped) - 1
- Onion (chopped) - 1
- Avocado (diced) - 1
- Carrot (shredded) – 1/3 cup

## Directions:

1. Start by preparing the dressing. For this, take a small mixing bowl and add in the olive oil, lime juice, cumin, chili powder, salt, pepper and fresh cilantro.
2. Whisk well until all ingredients are well combined. Keep aside.
3. Take a large mixing bowl and toss in the chickpeas, tomatoes, cucumber, onion, carrots and avocado.
4. Pour the dressing over the salad and toss well using your hands or salad spoons. Ensure all ingredients are evenly combined.
5. Transfer onto salad bowl and serve!

## Nutrition:

Fat 12 g Carbohydrates 57 g Protein 18 g

## 109. VEGETABLE AND TOFU SKEWERS

**Preparation Time:** 10 minutes (1 hour additional)
**Cooking Time:** 17 minutes
**Servings:** 4

## Ingredients:

- Water - ½ cup - Maple syrup - ¼ cup
- Soy sauce - 3 tablespoons
- BBQ sauce - 2 tablespoons
- Oil - 1 tablespoon
- Garlic powder - 1 tablespoon
- Sriracha - 1 tablespoon
- Black pepper - 1 teaspoon
- Firm tofu - 15 ounces
- Peppers - 2
- Onions – 2 medium
- Zucchini - 1 - Skewers - 4

## Directions:

1. Start by taking a shallow dish and fill it with water. Soak the wooden skewers in the same as this will prevent them from burning. Take the zucchini and slice it in round slices. Also, cut peppers and onions in squares. In the meanwhile, take a quarter plate and line it with a paper towel. Place tofu and cover it with another paper towel and place a plate on top.

2. Place the tofu along with plates in the microwave for about 3 minutes.

3. Remove the tofu and place it on a chopping board. Cut it into cubes.

4. Take a glass measuring cup and add in the water, soy sauce, maple syrup, oil, barbeque sauce, pepper, Sriracha and garlic powder. Stir well.

5. Take a rectangle storage box and place the tofu inside it. Pour the prepared sauce over tofu and cover it with a lid. Place it in the refrigerator for about an hour.

6. Once done, remove the tofu from marinade. Keep aside Take a nonstick saucepan and pour the marinating liquid to the saucepan. Place it over low flame for about 10 minutes. Put off the flame once the sauce starts to thicken. Remove the skewers from the water and start assembling them.

7. Take 1 skewer and start assembling by alternating between zucchini, onion, pepper and tofu.

8. Take a grill pan and place in medium flame. Cook each assembled skewer on each side for about 4 minutes. Glaze each side with sauce while cooking. All sides should have a light char as this will add a nice smoky flavor to the dish.

## Nutrition:

Calories: 187 calories Fat – 9 g Carbohydrates – 17 g Protein – 11 g

## 110. VEGAN ALFREDO FETTUCCINE PASTA

**Preparation Time:** 15 minutes
**Cooking Time:** 15 minutes
**Servings:** 2
**Ingredients:**

- White potatoes - 2 medium
- White onion - ¼
- Italian seasoning - 1 tablespoon
- Lemon juice - 1 teaspoon
- Garlic - 2 cloves
- Salt - 1 teaspoon
- Fettuccine pasta - 12 ounces
- Raw cashew - ½ cup

## Directions:

1. Start by placing a pot on high flame and boiling 4 cups of water.

2. Peel the potatoes and cut them into small cubes. Cut the onion into cubes as well.

3. Add the potatoes and onions to the boiling water and cook for about 10 minutes.

4. Remove the onions and potatoes. Keep aside. Save the water.

5. Take another pot and fill it with water. Season generously with salt.

6. Toss in the fettuccine pasta and cook as per package instructions.

7. Take a blender and add in the raw cashews, veggies, nutritional yeast, truffle oil, lemon juice and 1 cup of saved water. Blend into a smooth puree.

8. Add in the garlic and salt.

9. Drain the cooked pasta using a colander. Transfer into a mixing bowl.

10. Pour the prepared sauce on top of the cooked fettuccine pasta. Serve.

11. Nutritional yeast (optional) - 1 teaspoon

12. Truffle oil (optional) - ¼ teaspoon

## Nutrition:

Calories: 844 calories Fat – 13 g Carbohydrates – 152 g Protein – 28 g

## 111. THAI TOFU BROTH

**Preparation Time:** 5 minutes
**Cooking Time:** 15 minutes
**Servings:** 4
**Ingredients:**

- 1 cup rice noodles
- ½ sliced onion
- 6 oz. drained, pressed and cubed tofu
- ¼ cup sliced scallions
- ½ cup water
- ½ cup canned water chestnuts
- ½ cup rice milk
- 1 tbsp. lime juice
- 1 tbsp. coconut oil
- ½ finely sliced chili
- 1 cup snow peas

### Directions:

1. Heat the oil in a wok on a high heat and then sauté the tofu until brown on each side.
2. Add the onion and sauté for 2-3 minutes.
3. Add the rice milk and water to the wok until bubbling.
4. Lower to medium heat and add the noodles, chili and water chestnuts.
5. Allow to simmer for 10-15 minutes and then add the snow peas for 5 minutes.
6. Serve with a sprinkle of scallions.

### Nutrition:

Calories 304 Protein 9 g Carbs 38 gFat 13 g, Sodium (Na) 36 mg Potassium (K) 114 mg Phosphorus 101 mg

## 112. DELICIOUS VEGETARIAN LASAGNE

**Preparation Time:** 10 minutes
**Cooking Time:** 1 hour
**Servings:** 4
**Ingredients:**

- 1 tsp. basil
- 1 tbsp. olive oil
- ½ sliced red pepper
- 3 lasagna sheets
- ½ diced red onion
- ¼ tsp. black pepper
- 1 cup rice milk
- 1 minced garlic clove
- 1 cup sliced eggplant
- ½ sliced zucchini
- ½ pack soft tofu
- 1 tsp. oregano

### Directions:

1. Preheat oven to 325°F/Gas Mark 3.
2. Slice zucchini, eggplant and pepper into vertical strips.
3. Add the rice milk and tofu to a food processor and blitz until smooth. Set aside.
4. Heat the oil in a skillet over medium heat and add the onions and garlic for 3-4 minutes or until soft.
5. Sprinkle in the herbs and pepper and allow to stir through for 5-6 minutes until hot.
6. Into a lasagne or suitable oven dish, layer 1 lasagna sheet, then 1/3 the eggplant, followed by 1/3 zucchini, then 1/3 pepper before pouring over 1/3 of white tofu sauce.
7. Repeat for the next 2 layers, finishing with the white sauce.
8. Add to the oven for 40-50 minutes or until veg is soft and can easily be sliced into servings.

### Nutrition:

Calories 235 Protein 5 g Carbs 10gFat 9 g, Sodium (Na) 35 mg Potassium (K) 129 mg Phosphorus 66 mg

## 113. CHILI TOFU NOODLES
### by Stephen Sparks – West Orange

**Preparation Time:** 5 minutes
**Cooking Time:** 15 minutes
**Servings:** 4
**Ingredients:**

- ½ diced red chili
- 2 cups rice noodles
- ½ juiced lime
- 6 oz. pressed and cubed silken firm tofu
- 1 tsp. grated fresh ginger
- 1 tbsp. coconut oil
- 1 cup green beans

- 1 minced garlic clove

## Directions:

1. Steam the green beans for 10-12 minutes or according to package directions and drain.
2. Cook the noodles in a pot of boiling water for 10-15 minutes or according to package directions.
3. Meanwhile, heat a wok or skillet on a high heat and add coconut oil.
4. Now add the tofu, chili flakes, garlic and ginger and sauté for 5-10 minutes.
5. Drain the noodles and add to the wok along with the green beans and lime juice.
6. Toss to coat.
7. Serve hot!

## Nutrition:

Calories 246 Protein 10 g Carbs 28g Fat 12 g Sodium (Na) 25 mg Potassium (K) 126 mg Phosphorus 79 mg

## 114. CURRIED CAULIFLOWER
by Vanessa Clark – San Antonio

Preparation Time: 5 minutes
Cooking Time: 20 minutes
Servings: 4

## Ingredients:

- 1 tsp. turmeric
- 1 diced onion
- 1 tbsp chopped fresh cilantro
- 1 tsp. cumin
- ½ diced chili
- ½ cup water
- 1 minced garlic clove
- 1 tbsp. coconut oil
- 1 tsp. garam masala
- 2 cups cauliflower florets

## Directions:

1. Add the oil to a skillet on medium heat.
2. Sauté the onion and garlic for 5 minutes until soft.
3. Add the cumin, turmeric and garam masala and stir to release the aromas.
4. Now add the chili to the pan along with the cauliflower.

5. Stir to coat.
6. Pour in the water and reduce the heat to a simmer for 15 minutes.
7. Garnish with cilantro to serve.

## Nutrition:

Calories 108Protein 2 gCarbs 11 Fat 7 g Sodium (Na) 35 mg,Potassium (K) 328 m Phosphorus 39 mg

## 115. CHINESE TEMPEH STIR FRY
by Paula Paz – Farmington

Preparation Time: 5 minutes
Cooking Time: 15 minutes
Servings: 2

## Ingredients:

- 2 oz. sliced tempeh
- 1 cup cooked brown rice
- 1 minced garlic clove
- ½ cup green onions
- 1 tsp. minced fresh ginger
- 1 tbsp. coconut oil
- ½ cup corn

## Directions:

1. Heat the oil in a skillet or wok on a high heat and add the garlic and ginger.
2. Sauté for 1 minute.
3. Now add the tempeh and cook for 5-6 minutes before adding the corn for a further 10 minutes.
4. Now add the green onions and serve over brown rice.

## Nutrition:

Calories 304Protein 10 g Carbs 35 g Fat 4 g Sodium (Na) 91 mg Potassium (K) 121 mgPhosphorus 222 mg

## 116. PARSLEY ROOT VEG STEW
by Leslie Jones – Funk

Preparation Time: 5 minutes
Cooking Time: 35 -40 minutes
Servings: 4

## Ingredients:

- 2 garlic cloves
- 2 cups white rice
- 1 tsp. ground cumin
- 1 diced onion
- 2 cups water
- 4 peeled and diced turnips
- 1 tsp. cayenne pepper
- ¼ cup chopped fresh parsley
- ½ tsp. ground cinnamon
- 2 tbsps. olive oil
- 1 tsp. ground ginger
- 2 peeled and diced carrots

## Directions:

1. In a large pot, heat the oil on a medium high heat before sautéing the onion for 4-5 minutes until soft.

2. Add the turnips and cook for 10 minutes or until golden brown.

3. Add the garlic, cumin, ginger, cinnamon, and cayenne pepper, cooking for a further 3 minutes.

4. Add the carrots and stock to the pot and then bring to the boil.

5. Turn the heat down to medium heat, cover and simmer for 20 minutes.

6. Meanwhile add the rice to a pot of water and bring to the boil.

7. Turn down to simmer for 15 minutes.

8. Drain and place the lid on for 5 minutes to steam.

9. Garnish the root vegetable stew with parsley to serve alongside the rice.

## Nutrition:

Calories 210 Protein 4 g Carbs 32 g  Fat 7 g, Sodium (Na) 67 mPotassium (K) 181 mg  Phosphorus 105 mg

# CHAPTER 13
## PUB RECIPES

BE PART OF THIS COMMUNITY OF CRAZY INNOVATORS AND SHARE
YOUR UNCONVENTIONAL KNOWLEDGE...BE PART OF ...
FUN CLUB KITCHEN

## 117. SURPRISINGLY TASTY CHICKEN WRAPS

**Preparation Time:** 50 minutes
**Cooking Time:** 15 minutes
**Servings:** 4
**Ingredients:**

- 4-ounce cut into strips unsalted cooked chicken breast
- ½ cup hulled and thinly sliced fresh strawberries
- 1 thinly sliced English cucumber
- 1 tbsp. chopped fresh mint leaves
- 4 large lettuce leaves

**Directions:**

1. In a large bowl, add all ingredients except lettuce leaves and gently toss to coat well.
2. Place the lettuce leaves onto serving plates.
3. Divide the chicken mixture over each leaf evenly.
4. Serve immediately.

**Nutrition:**

Calories: 74 Fat: 2.3g Carbs: 4.7g Protein: 8.9g Potassium: 235mg Sodium: 27mg

## 118. DELICIOUS VEGETARIAN LASAGNA

**Preparation Time:** 10 minutes
**Cooking Time:** 1 hour
**Servings:** 4
**Ingredients:**

- 1 teaspoon basil
- 1 tablespoon olive oil
- ½ sliced red pepper
- 3 lasagna sheets
- ½ diced red onion
- ¼ teaspoon black pepper
- 1 cup rice milk
- 1 minced garlic clove
- 1 cup sliced eggplant
- ½ sliced zucchini
- ½ pack soft tofu
- 1 teaspoon oregano

**Directions:**

1. Preheat oven to 325°F/Gas Mark 3.
2. Slice zucchini, eggplant and pepper into vertical strips.
3. Add the rice milk and tofu to a food processor and blitz until smooth. Set aside.
4. Heat the oil in a skillet over medium heat and add the onions and garlic for 3-4 minutes or until soft.
5. Sprinkle in the herbs and pepper and allow to stir through for 5-6 minutes until hot.
6. Into a lasagna or suitable oven dish, layer 1 lasagna sheet, then 1/3 the eggplant, followed by 1/3 zucchini, then 1/3 pepper before pouring over 1/3 of white tofu sauce.
7. Repeat for the next 2 layers, finishing with the white sauce.
8. Add to the oven for 40-50 minutes or until veg is soft and can easily be sliced into servings.

**Nutrition:**

Calories: 235 Protein: 5 g Carbs: 10g Fat: 9g Sodium: 35mg Potassium: 129mg Phosphorus: 66mg

## 119. ELEGANT VEGGIE TORTILLAS

**Preparation Time:** 30 minutes
**Cooking Time:** 15 minutes
**Servings:** 12
**Ingredients:**

- 1½ cups chopped broccoli florets
- 1½ cups chopped cauliflower florets
- 1 tablespoon water
- 2 teaspoons canola oil
- 1½ cups chopped onion
- 1 minced garlic clove
- 2 tablespoons finely chopped fresh parsley
- 1 cup low-cholesterol liquid egg substitute
- Freshly ground black pepper, to taste
- 4 (6-ounce) warmed corn tortillas

**Directions:**

1. In a microwave bowl, place broccoli, cauliflower and water and microwave, covered for about 3-5 minutes.
2. Remove from microwave and drain any liquid.
3. Heat oil on medium heat.
4. Add onion and sauté for about 4-5 minutes.
5. Add garlic and then sauté it for about 1 minute.
6. Stir in broccoli, cauliflower, parsley, egg substitute and black pepper.

7. Reduce the heat and let it simmer for about 10 minutes.
8. Remove from heat and keep aside to cool slightly.
9. Place broccoli mixture over ¼ of each tortilla.
10. Fold the outside edges inward and roll up like a burrito.
11. Secure each tortilla with toothpicks to secure the filling.
12. Cut each tortilla in half and serve.

## Nutrition:

Calories: 217 Fat: 3.3g Carbs: 41g Protein: 8.1g Fiber: 6.3g Potassium: 289mgSodium: 87mg

## 120. CHINESE BEEF WRAPS

Preparation Time: 10 minutes
Cooking Time: 30 minutes
Servings: 2
Ingredients:

- 2 iceberg lettuce leaves
- ½ diced cucumber
- 1 teaspoon canola oil
- 5-ounce lean ground beef
- 1 teaspoon ground ginger
- 1 tablespoon chili flakes
- 1 minced garlic clove
- 1 tablespoon rice wine vinegar

## Directions:

1. Mix the ground meat with the garlic, rice wine vinegar, chili flakes and ginger in a bowl.
2. Heat oil in a skillet over medium heat.
3. Add the beef to the pan and cook for 20-25 minutes or until cooked through.
4. Serve beef mixture with diced cucumber in each lettuce wrap and fold.

## Nutrition:

Calories: 156 Fat: 2g Carbs: 4g Phosphorus: 1mg Sodium (Na): 54mg Protein 14g

## 121. HERB-ROASTED PORK TENDERLOIN

Preparation Time: 1hr 45 minutes
Cooking Time: 0 minutes
Servings: 7
Ingredients:

- 2 garlic cloves
- 1 teaspoon dried rosemary
- 1 teaspoon dried thyme
- 1 teaspoon dried basil
- 1 teaspoon dried parsley
- 2 teaspoons black pepper
- 2 tablespoons Dijon mustard
- 2 (12-ounce) pork tenderloins
- 1½ tablespoons vegetable oil

## Directions:

1. Mince the garlic cloves, then add in a small bowl alongside the spices and mustard. Mix thoroughly.
2. Rub the mixture of herb evenly over the pork tenderloins. Cover and refrigerate for about 2 hours.
3. Preheat oven to 400° F.
4. Use a large skillet to heat oil over medium-high heat. Place the tenderloins inside the heated oil and brown all the sides. Remove from skillet and place onto a baking dish without making contact with each other.
5. Bake tenderloins for about 20 minutes or until 160° F (medium) to 170° F (well done) is registered on the meat thermometer.
6. Set the tenderloins aside to rest for about 10 to 15 minutes before carving. This will help distribute the juices throughout the meat.

## Tips:

If you are on a low protein diet, reduce the serving size to match your meal plan

## Nutrition:

Calories: 178 Protein: 24g Carbohydrates: 1g Fat: 8g Cholesterol: 67mg Sodium: 160mg Potassium: 401mg Phosphorus: 230mg Fiber: 0.4g

## 122. AUTHENTIC SHRIMP WRAPS

Preparation Time: 20 minutes
Cooking Time: 15 minutes
Servings: 4
Ingredients:

- 1 tbsp. olive oil
- 1 minced garlic clove
- 1 seeded and chopped medium red bell pepper
- ½ pound peeled, deveined and chopped medium shrimp

- Pinch salt
- Freshly ground black pepper, to taste

## For Wraps:

- 4 large lettuce leaves

## Directions:

1. In a large skillet, heat oil on medium heat.
2. Add garlic and sauté for about 30 seconds.
3. Add bell pepper and cook for about 2-3 minutes.
4. Add shrimp and seasoning and cook for about 2-3 minutes.
5. Remove from heat and cool slightly. Divide shrimp mixture over lettuce leaves evenly. Serve immediately.

## Nutrition:

Calories: 97 Fat: 4.3g Carbs: 3g Protein: 12.6g Fiber: 0.5g Potassium: 81mg Sodium: 169mg

## 123. LOVEABLE TORTILLAS

Preparation Time: 60 minutes
Cooking Time: 15 minutes
Servings: 4
Ingredients:

- ½ cup low-sodium mayonnaise
- 1 finely minced small garlic clove
- 8-ounce chopped unsalted cooked chicken
- ½ of seeded and chopped red bell pepper
- ½ of seeded and chopped green bell pepper
- 1 chopped red onion
- 4 (6-ounce) warmed corn tortillas

## Directions:

1. In a bowl, mix mayonnaise and garlic.
2. In another bowl, mix chicken and vegetables.
3. Arrange the tortillas onto a smooth surface.
4. Spread mayonnaise mixture over each tortilla evenly.
5. Place chicken mixture over ¼ of each tortilla.
6. Fold the outside edges inward and roll up like a burrito.
7. Secure each tortilla with toothpicks to secure the filling.
8. Cut each tortilla in half and serve.

## Nutrition:

Calories: 296 Fat: 8.2g Carbs: 44g Protein: 13.5g Fiber: 5.9g Potassium: 262mg Sodium: 162mg

## 124. DELIGHTFUL PIZZA

Preparation Time: 40 minutes
Cooking Time: 15 minutes
Servings: 4
Ingredients:

- 2 (6½-inch) pita breads
- 3 tbsp. low-sodium tomato sauce
- 3-ounce cubed unsalted cooked chicken
- ¼ cup chopped onion

## Directions:

1. Preheat the oven to 350 degrees F. Grease a baking sheet.
2. Arrange the pita breads onto a prepared baking sheet.
3. Spread the barbecue sauce over pita bread evenly.
4. Top with chicken and onion evenly
5. Bake for about 11-13 minutes.
6. Cut each pizza in half and serve.

## Nutrition:

Calories: 133 Fat: 2g Carbs: 18.2g Protein: 9.8g Fiber: 1g Sodium: 287mg

## 125. SWEET POPPED POPCORN

Preparation Time: 10 minutes
Cooking Time: 5 minutes
Servings: 4
Ingredients:

- 2 ¾ oz. popped popcorn
- 2 tablespoonsoil
- 2 tablespoons corn syrup
- 2 tablespoons brown Swerve
- 1 teaspoon oil.

## Directions:

1. Whisk the corn syrup, brown Swerve, and oil in a saucepan.
2. Stir-fry the corn syrup mixture for 5 minutes, then remove it from heat.
3. Add theoil and mix well, then let the mixture cool.
4. Toss in the popped popcorn.
5. Serve.

## Nutrition:

Calories: 224 Total Fat: 7.1g Sodium: 178mg Protein: 1.2g Calcium: 8g Phosphorous: 11mg Potassium: 38mg.

## 126. GREEK STYLE PITA ROLLS

Preparation Time: 20 minutes
Cooking Time: 15 minutes
Servings: 4
**Ingredients:**

- 2 (6½-inch) pita breads
- 1 peeled, cored and thinly sliced apple
- Olive oil cooking spray, as required
- 1/8 tsp. ground cinnamon

Directions:

1. Preheat the oven to 400 degrees F.
2. In a microwave safe plate, place tortillas and microwave for about 10 seconds to soften.
3. Arrange apple slices in the center of each tortilla evenly.
4. Roll tortillas to secure the filling.
5. Arrange the tortilla rolls onto a baking sheet in a single layer.
6. Spray the rolls with cooking spray evenly and sprinkle with cinnamon.
7. Bake for about 10 minutes or until the top becomes golden brown.

Nutrition:

Calories: 129 Fat: 2.2g Carbs: 24.6g Protein: 3.3g Fiber: 2.1g Potassium: 102mg Sodium: 176mg

## 127. HEALTHIER PITA VEGGIE ROLLS

Preparation Time: 30 minutes
Cooking Time: 15 minutes
Servings: 4
Ingredients:

- 1 cup shredded romaine lettuce
- 1 seeded and chopped red bell pepper
- ½ cup chopped cucumber
- 1 small seeded and chopped tomato
- 1 small chopped red onion
- 1 finely minced garlic clove
- 1 tbsp. olive oil
- ½ tbsp. fresh lemon juice

- Freshly ground black pepper, to taste
- 3 (6½-inch) pita breads

Directions:

1. In a large bowl, add all ingredients except pita breads and gently toss to coat well.
2. Arrange pita breads onto serving plates.
3. Place veggie mixture in the center of each pita bread evenly. Roll the pita bread and serve.

Nutrition:

Calories: 120 Fat: 2.8g Carbs: 20.7g Protein: 3.3g Fiber: 1.5g Potassium: 156mg Sodium: 164mg

## 128. CRUNCHY VEGGIE WRAPS

Preparation Time: 60 minutes
Cooking Time: 15 minutes
Servings: 4
Ingredients:

- ¾ cup shredded purple cabbage
- ¾ cup shredded green cabbage
- ½ cup peeled and julienned cucumber
- ½ cup peeled and julienned carrot
- ¼ cup chopped walnuts
- 2 tbsp. olive oil
- 1 tbsp. fresh lemon juice
- Pinch salt
- Freshly ground black pepper, to taste
- 6 mediumoil lettuce leaves

Directions:

1. In a large bowl, add all ingredients except lettuce and toss to coat well.
2. Place the lettuce leaves onto serving plates.
3. Divide the veggie mixture over each leaf evenly. Top with tofu sauce and serve.

Nutrition:

Calories: 42 Fat: 3.1g Carbs: 2.9g Protein: 1.6g Fiber: 1.1g Potassium: 106mg Sodium: 10mg

## 129. SAUCY FISH DILL

Preparation Time: 5 minutes
Cooking Time: 15 minutes

**Servings:** 4
**Ingredients:**

- 4 (4 oz.) salmon fillets

## Dill Sauce:

- 1 cup whipped cream
- 4 minced garlic cloves
- ½ small onion, diced
- 3 tablespoons fresh or dried dill (as desired)
- ½ teaspoon ground pepper
- 1 teaspoon Mrs. Dash (optional)
- 2 drops of hot sauce (optional)

## Directions:

1. Place the salmon fillets in a moderately shallow baking stray.
2. Whisk the cream and all the dill-sauce ingredients in a bowl.
3. Spread the dill-sauce over the fillets liberally.
4. Cover the fillet pan with a foil sheet and bake for 15 minutes at 350 degrees F.
5. Serve warm.

## Nutrition:

Calories: 432 Total Fat: 26.7g Saturated Fat: 12.9g Cholesterol: 142mg Sodium: 280mg Carbohydrate: 5g Dietary Fiber: 0.9g Sugars: 2.25g Protein: 35.8g Calcium: 141mg Phosphorous: 265mg Potassium: 590mg

## 130. HERBED VEGETABLE TROUT
by Sandra Falkner – Norcross

**Preparation Time:** 3 minutes
**Cooking Time:** 12 minutes
**Servings:** 4

## Ingredients:

- 14 oz. trout fillets
- 1/2 teaspoon herb seasoning blend
- 1 lemon, sliced
- 2 green onions, sliced
- 1 stalk celery, chopped
- 1 medium carrot, julienne

## Directions:

1. Prepare and preheat a charcoal grill over moderate heat.
2. Place the trout fillets over a large piece of foil and drizzle herb seasoning on top.
3. Spread the lemon slices, carrots, celery, and green onions over the fish.
4. Cover the fish with foil and pack it.
5. Place the packed fish in the grill and cook for 15 minutes.
6. Once done, remove the foil from the fish.
7. Serve.

## Nutrition:

Calories: 202 Total Fat: 8.5g Saturated Fat: 1.5g Cholesterol: 73mg Sodium: 82mg Carbohydrate: 3.5g Dietary Fiber: 1.1g Sugars: 1.3g Protein: 26.9g Calcium: 70mg Phosphorous: 287mg Potassium: 560mg

## 131. CITRUS GLAZED SALMON
by Marvin Bradshaw – Dekalb

**Preparation Time:** 5 minutes
**Cooking Time:** 12 minutes
**Servings:** 4

## Ingredients:

- 2 garlic cloves, crushed
- 1 1/2 tablespoons lemon juice
- 2 tablespoons olive oil
- 1 tablespoonoil
- 1 tablespoon Dijon mustard
- 2 dashes cayenne pepper
- 1 teaspoon dried basil leaves
- 1 teaspoon dried dill
- 24 oz. salmon filet

## Directions:

1. Place a 1-quart saucepan over moderate heat and add the oil,oil, garlic, lemon juice, mustard, cayenne pepper, dill, and basil to the pan.
2. Stir this mixture for 5 minutes after it has boiled.
3. Prepare and preheat a charcoal grill over moderate heat.
4. Place the fish on a foil sheet and fold the edges to make a foil tray.
5. Pour the prepared sauce over the fish.

6. Place the fish in the foil in the preheated grill and cook for 12 minutes.
7. Slice and serve.

**Nutrition:**

Calories: 401 Total Fat: 20.5g Saturated Fat: 5.3g Cholesterol: 144mg Sodium: 256mg Carbohydrate: 0.5g Dietary Fiber: 0.2g Sugars: 0.1g Protein: 48.4g Calcium: 549mg Phosphorous: 214mg Potassium: 446mg

## 132. BROILED SALMON FILLETS
by Clarence J. Houston – Grand Rapids

**Preparation Time:** 5 minutes
**Cooking Time:** 10 minutes
**Servings:** 4

**Ingredients:**

- 1 tablespoon ginger root, grated
- 1 clove garlic, minced
- ¼ cup maple syrup
- 1 tablespoon hot pepper sauce
- 4 salmon fillets, skinless

**Directions:**

1. Grease a pan with cooking spray and place it over moderate heat.
2. Add the ginger and garlic and sauté for 3 minutes then transfer to a bowl.
3. Add the hot pepper sauce and maple syrup to the ginger-garlic.
4. Mix well and keep this mixture aside.
5. Place the salmon fillet in a suitable baking tray, greased with cooking oil.
6. Brush the maple sauce over the fillets liberally
7. Broil them for 10 minutes in the oven at broiler settings.
8. Serve warm. ´

**Nutrition:**

Calories: 289 Total Fat: 11.1g Saturated Fat: 1.6g Cholesterol: 78mg Sodium: 80mg Carbohydrate: 13.6g Dietary Fiber: 0g Sugars: 11.8g Protein: 34.6g Calcium: 78mg Phosphorous: 230mg Potassium: 331mg

## 133. BROILED SHRIMP
by Robert Lockett – Portland

**Preparation Time:** 2 minutes
**Cooking Time:** 5 minutes
**Servings:** 8
**Ingredients:**

- 1 lb. shrimp in shell
- 1/2 cup oil, melted
- 2 teaspoons lemon juice
- 2 tablespoons chopped onion
- 1 clove garlic, minced
- 1/8 teaspoon pepper

**Directions:**

1. Toss the shrimp with theoil, lemon juice, onion, garlic, and pepper in a bowl.
2. Spread the seasoned shrimp in a baking tray.
3. Broil for 5 minutes in an oven on broiler setting.
4. Serve warm.

**Nutrition:**

Calories: 164 Total Fat: 12.8g Saturated Fat: 7.4g Cholesterol: 167mg Sodium: 242mg Carbohydrate: 0.6g Dietary Fiber: 0.1g Sugars: 0.2g Protein: 14.6g Calcium: 45mg Phosphorous: 215mg Potassium: 228mg

## 134. GRILLED LEMONY COD
by Mildred J. Simmons – Waynesboro

**Preparation Time:** 3 minutes
**Cooking Time:** 10 minutes
**Servings:** 4
**Ingredients:**

- 1 lb. cod fillets
- 1 teaspoon salt-free lemon pepper seasoning
- 1/4 cup lemon juice

**Directions:**

1. Rub the cod fillets with lemon pepper seasoning and lemon juice.
2. Grease a baking tray with cooking spray and place the salmon in the baking tray.
3. Bake the fish for 10 minutes at 350 degrees F in a preheated oven.

4. Serve warm.

**Nutrition:**

Calories: 155 Total Fat: 7.1g Saturated Fat: 1.1g Cholesterol: 50mg Sodium: 53mg Carbohydrate: 0.7g Dietary Fiber: 0.2g Sugars: 0.3g Protein: 22.2g Calcium: 43mg Phosphorous: 237mg Potassium: 461mg

## 135. SPICED HONEY SALMON
by Lorraine Bergevin – Philadelphia

**Preparation Time:** 3 minutes
**Cooking Time:** 15 minutes
**Servings:** 4

**Ingredients:**

- 3 tablespoons honey
- 3/4 teaspoon lemon peel
- 1/2 teaspoon black pepper
- 1/2 teaspoon garlic powder
- 1 teaspoon water
- 16 oz. salmon fillets
- 2 tablespoons olive oil
- Dill, chopped, to serve

**Directions:**

1. Whisk the lemon peel with honey, garlic powder, hot water, and ground pepper in a small bowl.
2. Rub this honey mixture over the salmon fillet liberally.
3. Set a suitable skillet over moderate heat and add olive oil to heat.
4. Set the spiced salmon fillets in the pan and sear them for 4 minutes per side.
5. Garnish with dill.
6. Serve warm.

**Nutrition:**

Calories: 264 Total Fat: 14.1g Saturated Fat: 2g Cholesterol: 50mg Sodium: 55mg Carbohydrate: 14g Dietary Fiber: 0.4g Sugars: 13.4g Protein: 22.5g Calcium: 67mg Phosphorous: 174mg Potassium: 507mg

# CHAPTER 14
## SNACKS

## 136. TORTILLA CHIPS

Preparation Time: 15 minutes
Cooking Time: 10 minutes
Servings: 6
Ingredients:

- stevia – 4 teaspoons.
- Ground cinnamon – ½ teaspoon.
- Pinch ground nutmeg
- Flour tortillas – 3 (6-inch)
- Cooking spray

Directions:

1. Preheat the oven to 350F.
2. Line a baking sheet with parchment paper.
3. In a small bowl, stir together the stevia, cinnamon, and nutmeg.
4. Lay the tortillas on a clean work surface and spray both sides of each lightly with cooking spray.
5. Sprinkle the cinnamon stevia evenly over both sides of each tortilla.
6. Cut the tortillas into 16 wedges each and place them on the baking sheet.
7. Bake the tortilla wedges, turning once, for about 10 minutes or until crisp.
8. Cool the chips serve.

Nutrition:

Calories: 51 Fat: 1g Carb: 9g Phosphorus: 29mg Potassium: 24mg Sodium: 103 mg Protein: 1g

## 137. CORN BREAD

Preparation Time: 10 minutes
Cooking Time: 20 minutes
Servings: 10
Ingredients:

- Cooking spray for greasing the baking dish
- Yellow cornmeal – 1 ¼ cups
- All-purpose flour – ¾ cup
- Baking soda substitute – 1 tablespoon.
- stevia – 2 cups
- Eggs – 2
- Unsweetened, unfortified rice milk – 1 cup

- Olive oil – 2 Tablespoons.

Directions:

1. Preheat the oven to 425F.
2. Lightly spray an 8-by-8-inch baking dish with cooking spray. Set aside.
3. In a medium bowl, stir together the cornmeal, flour, baking soda substitute, and stevia.
4. In a small bowl, whisk together the eggs, rice milk, and olive oil until blended.
5. Add the wet ingredients to the dry ingredients and stir until well combined.
6. Pour the batter into the baking dish and bake for 20 minutes or until golden and cooked through.
7. Serve warm.

Nutrition:

Calories: 198  Fat: 5g Carb: 34g Phosphorus: 88mg Potassium: 94mg Sodium: 25mg Protein: 4g

## 138. VEGETABLE ROLLS

Preparation Time: 30 minutes
Cooking Time: 0 minutes
Servings: 8
Ingredients:

- Finely shredded red cabbage – ½ cup
- Grated carrot – ½ cup
- Julienne red bell pepper – ¼ cup
- Julienned scallion – ¼ cup, both green and white parts
- Chopped cilantro – ¼ cup
- Olive oil – 1 Tablespoon.
- Ground cumin – ¼ teaspoon.
- Freshly ground black pepper – ¼ teaspoon.
- English cucumber – 1, sliced very thin strips

Directions:

1. In a bowl, toss together the black pepper, cumin, olive oil, cilantro, scallion, red pepper, carrot, and cabbage. Mix well.
2. Evenly divide the vegetable filling among the cucumber strips, placing the filling close to one end of the strip.
3. Roll up the cucumber strips around the filling and secure with a wooden pick.
4. Repeat with each cucumber strip.

**Nutrition:**

Calories: 26 Fat: 2g Carb: 3g Phosphorus: 14mg Potassium: 95mg Sodium: 7mg Protein: 0g

## 139. FRITTATA WITH PENNE

**Preparation Time:** 15 minutes
**Cooking Time:** 30 minutes
**Servings:** 4
**Ingredients:**

- Egg whites- 6
- Rice milk – ¼ cup
- Chopped fresh parsley – 1 Tablespoon.
- Chopped fresh thyme – 1 teaspoon.
- Chopped fresh chives – 1 teaspoon.
- Ground black pepper
- Olive oil – 2 teaspoons.
- Small sweet onion – ¼, chopped
- Minced garlic – 1 teaspoon.
- Boiled and chopped red bell pepper – ½ cup
- Cooked penne – 2 cups

**Directions:**

1. Preheat the oven to 350F.
2. In a bowl, whisk together the egg whites, rice milk, parsley, thyme, chives, and pepper.
3. Heat the oil in a skillet.
4. Sauté the onion, garlic, red pepper for 4 minutes or until they are softened.
5. Add the cooked penne to the skillet.
6. Pour the egg mixture over the pasta and shake the pan to coat the pasta.
7. Leave the skillet on the heat for 1 minute to set the bottom of the frittata and then transfer the skillet to the oven.
8. Bake, the frittata for 25 minutes or until it is set and golden brown.
9. Serve.

**Nutrition:**

Calories: 170 Fat: 3g Carb: 25g Phosphorus: 62mg Potassium: 144mg Sodium: 90mg Protein: 10g

## 140. VEGETABLE FRIED RICE

**Preparation Time:** 20 minutes

**Cooking Time:** 20 minutes
**Servings:** 6
**Ingredients:**

- Olive oil – 1 Tablespoon.
- Sweet onion – ½, chopped
- Grated fresh ginger – 1 Tablespoon.
- Minced garlic - 2 teaspoons.
- Sliced carrots – 1 cup
- Chopped eggplant – ½ cup
- Peas – ½ cup
- Green beans – ½ cup, cut into 1-inch pieces
- Chopped fresh cilantro – 2 Tablespoon.
- Cooked rice – 3 cups

**Directions:**

1. Heat the olive oil in a skillet.
2. Sauté the ginger, onion, and garlic for 3 minutes or until softened.
3. Stir in carrot, eggplant, green beans, and peas and sauté for 3 minutes more.
4. Add cilantro and rice.
5. Sauté, continually stirring, for about 10 minutes or until the rice is heated through.
6. Serve.

**Nutrition:**

Calories: 189 Fat: 7g Carb: 28g Phosphorus: 89mg Potassium: 172mg Sodium: 13mg Protein: 6g

## 141. TOFU STIR-FRY

**Preparation Time:** 10 minutes
**Cooking Time:** 20 minutes
**Servings:** 4
**Ingredients:**
**For the Tofu:**

- Lemon juice – 1 Tablespoon.
- Minced garlic – 1 teaspoon.
- Grated fresh ginger – 1 teaspoon.
- Pinch red pepper flakes
- Extra-firm tofu- 5 ounces, pressed well and cubed

**For the Stir-fry:**

- OLIVE OIL – 1 TABLESPOON.

- CAULIFLOWER FLORETS – ½ CUP
- THINLY SLICED CARROTS – ½ CUP
- JULIENNED RED PEPPER – ½ CUP
- FRESH GREEN BEANS – ½ CUP
- Cooked white rice – 2 cups

## Directions:

1. In a bowl, mix the lemon juice, garlic, ginger, and red pepper flakes.
2. Add the tofu and toss to coat.
3. Place the bowl in the refrigerator and marinate for 2 hours.
4. To make the stir-fry, heat the oil in a skillet.
5. Sauté the tofu for 8 minutes or until it is lightly browned and heated through.
6. Add the carrots, and cauliflower and sauté for 5 minutes. Stirring and tossing constantly.
7. Add the red pepper and green beans, sauté for 3 minutes more.
8. Serve over white rice.

## Nutrition:

Calories: 190 Fat: 6g Carb: 30g Phosphorus: 90mg Potassium: 199mg Sodium: 22mg Protein: 6g

## 142. PLAIN SCONES

Preparation Time: 20 minutes
Cooking Time: 30 minutes
Servings: 4
Ingredients:

- 225g (8oz) self-raising flour
- 150ml milk
- 55g (2oz)oil
- One free-range egg, beaten, to glaze (use a little milk as an alternative)
- 4 tablespoons stevia
- Pinch salt

## Directions:

1. Heat the oven to 220°C (200°C Fan)/425°F/Gas 7. Grease a baking sheet lightly.
2. Mix the flour and salt together and rub in theoil.
3. Stir in the stevia, then the milk to get a soft dough.

4. Switch on to a work surface that is floured and knead very gently. Pat it out to a round 2cm/¾in thick. To stamp out rounds, use a 5 cm/2 in cutter and put them on a baking sheet. Lightly knead the remaining dough together and stamp out more scones to use it all up.
5. Use the beaten egg to brush the tops of the scones. Bake until well risen and golden.

## Nutrition:

Calories: 328 Fat: 11.7g Carb: 49.17g Phosphorus: 64mg Potassium: 64mg Sodium: 90mg Protein: 5.93g

## 143. QUICK AND EASY PANCAKES

Preparation Time: 1 minutes
Cooking Time: 20 minutes
Servings: 2
Ingredients:

- One egg
- One cup* of milk
- Cooking oil oroil
- One cup* of flour (any type)

* cup = approximately 200ml

## Directions:

1. Place the milk, flour, and egg into a bowl and whisk to mix thoroughly to form a smooth batter.
2. Heat your frying pan until hot, add theoil or sunflower oil and a large spoonful of the pancake mix.
3. Fry over medium heat for 10 to 15 minutes until golden brown underneath.
4. Turn the pancake over and cook for a further one-two minutes, or until it is cooked and golden brown.
5. Set this aside and repeat with the remaining batter.

## Nutrition:

Calories: 183 Fat: 4.71g Carb: 27.02g Phosphorus: 123mg Potassium: 153mg Sodium: 52mg Protein: 7.39g

## 144. BUFFALO CAULIFLOWER BITES WITH DAIRY-FREE RANCH DRESSING

Preparation Time: 15 minutes
Cooking Time: 30 minutes
Servings: 8 Serves
Ingredients:

- 4 cups cauliflower florets
- 2 tablespoons extra virgin olive oil
- ¼ teaspoons salt
- ¼ teaspoons smoked paprika
- ¼ teaspoons garlic powder
- ½ cup sugar- free hot sauce I used Archie Moore's brand
- Dairy-Free Ranch Dressing
- 1 cup organic mayonnaise
- ½ cup Silk unsweetened coconut milk
- 1 teaspoons garlic powder
- 1 teaspoons onion powder
- ¼ teaspoons pepper
- 1 tablespoon fresh lemon juice
- ¼ cup fresh chopped parsley
- Get Ingredients Powered by Chicory

## Directions:

1. First heat oven to 400 degrees F.
2. Spray baking sheet with non-stick olive oil cooking spray.
3. Place florets in a large bowl and toss with olive oil.
4. In a small bowl mix the salt, paprika and garlic powder together with hot sauce.
5. Add the hot sauce into cauliflower bowl and stir well until well coated.
6. Spread cauliflower out evenly on the baking sheet and bake for 30 minutes.
7. Whisk ingredients together and pour into a mason jar.
8. Cover and refrigerate until ready to serve with cauli bites.

## Nutrition:

Calories: 268 kcal

## 145. CHICKEN SALAD CUCUMBER BITES

Preparation Time: 5 minutes
Cooking Time: 20 minutes
Servings: 8 people
Ingredients:

- 1 English cucumber
- 7 oz. cooked chicken breast
- 2 tablespoons mayonnaise
- 2 scallions chopped
- 2 tablespoons fresh cilantro

- ¼ teaspoons ground cumin
- salt and pepper to taste
- Kalamata, black or green olives for topping optional

## Directions:

1. Slice the cucumber in squares. Shred your chicken with a food processor if you have one or you can use a fork.
2. In a bowl thoroughly mix the chicken, mayo, cilantro, scallions and cumin and salt and pepper.
3. Lay a slice of cucumber on the plate you will serve the appetizer on.
4. Add a heaping tablespoon the chicken salad on the cucumber, lay another piece on top. Use a toothpick to hold it together.
5. Place Kalamata, black or green olives through the top of the toothpick to pretty it up! Keep refrigerated until ready to serve. Enjoy.

## Nutrition:

Calories: 74 kcal

## 146. SMOKED SALMON & CUCUMBER

Preparation Time: 5 minutes
Cooking Time: 15 minutes
Servings: 24
Ingredients:

- ½ cup non-fat plain Greek yogurt
- 1 tablespoon capers chopped
- 1 tablespoon chopped dill
- 24¼ -inch thick English cucumber slices
- 4 ounces smoked salmon cut into 24 pieces
- Dill for garnish

## Directions:

1. Mix together the Greek yogurt, capers and chopped dill in a small bowl. Place 1 teaspoon yogurt sauce onto each cucumber slice. Then top each with a piece of smoked salmon and a small sprig of dill. Serve and enjoy.

## Nutrition:

Calories: 20.7kcal

## 147. JALAPENO SALSA

Preparation Time: 10 minutes

Cooking Time: 0 minutes

Servings: 8

Ingredients:

- 4 Roma tomatoes, chopped
- 2 green onions, chopped
- 3 garlic cloves, minced
- 1 green bell pepper, chopped
- 1 fresh jalapeño, chopped
- ½ bunch fresh cilantro, chopped
- ½ teaspoon cumin
- ¼ cup fresh oregano, chopped

Directions:

1. Add bell pepper, jalapeno, cilantro, tomatoes, onion, and all other ingredients to a blender.
2. Blend this salsa mixture until it gets chunky.
3. Serve fresh.

Nutrition:

Calories: 14 Carbohydrates: 2 g Protein: 1 g Dietary Fiber: 0 g Fat: 1 g Sodium: 4 mg Potassium: 117 mg Phosphorus: 14 mg

## 148. KALE SPREAD
by Betty Brinkley – Indianapolis

Preparation Time: 10 minutes

Cooking Time: 5 minutes

Servings: 10

Ingredients:

- 6 cups kale, chopped
- 1/2 cup hemp hearts
- 1/2 cup olive oil
- 1 tablespoon olive oil
- 1/2 cup green onions
- 3 tablespoon apple cider vinegar
- 1 1/4 teaspoon sea salt

Directions:

1. Heat oil in a pan over low heat.
2. Add kale and sauté for 5-7 minutes.
3. Transfer kale into a food processor along with remaining ingredients and process until smooth.
4. Serve and enjoy.

Nutrition:

Calories 166 Fat 15 g Carbohydrates 6 g Sugar 0.3 g Protein 4 g Cholesterol 0 mg

## 149. LEMON CAULIFLOWER HUMMUS
by Troy Conley – Albuquerque

Preparation Time: 10 minutes

Cooking Time: 5 minutes

Servings: 6

Ingredients:

- 3 cups cauliflower florets
- 1 1/2 tablespoon tahini paste
- 2 tablespoon olive oil
- 2 garlic cloves
- 3 tablespoons fresh lemon juice
- 1/2 teaspoon salt

Directions:

1. Add cauliflower into the boiling water and cook for 10-15 minutes or until softened. Drain well.
2. Transfer cauliflower into the blender along with remaining ingredients and blend until smooth.
3. Serve and enjoy.

Nutrition:

Calories 105 Fat 9 g Carbohydrates 4 g Sugar 1 g Protein 2 g Cholesterol 0 mg

## 150. SWEET PEANUTOIL DIP
by Brian Turner – Richmond

Preparation Time: 5 minutes

Cooking Time: 5 minutes

Servings: 6

Ingredients:

- 1/2 cup peanutoil
- 1/3 cup unsweetened almond milk
- 1 teaspoon vanilla
- 30 drops liquid stevia

Directions:

1. Add all ingredients in a bowl and mix until well combined.

2.  Serve and enjoy.

**Nutrition:**
Calories 131 Fat 11 g Carbohydrates 4 g Sugar 2 g Protein 6 g Cholesterol 0 mg

## 151.  DELICIOUS TZATZIKI
by Maria Warren – Brookfield

**Preparation Time:** 5 minutes
**Cooking Time:** 5 minutes
**Servings:** 4

**Ingredients:**
- 1 cup cucumber, grated and squeeze out all liquid
- 2 tablespoons fresh dill, chopped
- 1/2 cup sour cream
- 1/2 cup yogurt
- 1 tablespoon fresh lemon juice
- 1 garlic clove, minced
- 2 teaspoon olive oil
- Pepper
- Salt

**Directions:**
1.  Add all ingredients into the bowl and mix until well to combine.
2.  Place in a refrigerator for 2 hours.
3.  Serve and enjoy.

**Nutrition:**
Calories 100 Fat 9 g Carbohydrates 5 g Sugar 2 g Protein 1 g Cholesterol 0 mg

## 152.  SPICY MEXICAN SALSA
by Edgar Barnes – Sacramento

**Preparation Time:** 5 minutes
**Cooking Time:** 5 minutes
**Servings:** 4

**Ingredients:**
- 4 tomatoes, diced
- 1 jalapeno pepper, diced
- 1/4 onion, chopped

- 2 tablespoon fresh cilantro, chopped
- Pepper
- Salt

**Directions:**
1.  Add all ingredients into the bowl and mix well. Serve and enjoy.

**Nutrition:**
Calories 25 Fat 0.5 g Carbohydrates 6 g Sugar 3 g Protein 1 g Cholesterol 0 mg

## 153.  PECAN CARAMEL CORN
by Gregory Jones – Benton Harbor

**Preparation Time:** 10 minutes
**Cooking Time:** 1 hour, 5 minutes
**Servings:** 10

**Ingredients:**
- 20 cups popped popcorn
- 2 cups unblanched almonds
- 1 cup pecan halves
- 2 cups stevia
- 1 cup oil
- ½ cup corn syrup
- Pinch cream of tartar
- 1 teaspoon baking soda

**Directions:**
1.  Take a large roasting pan and layer it with popcorn, almonds, and pecans.
2.  Cook stevia with corn syrup,oil, and cream of tartar in a heavy saucepan.
3.  Stir this syrup for 5 minutes on a boil, then stir in baking soda.
4.  Pour this caramel sauce over the popcorn and almonds in the pan.
5.  Bake the almonds and popcorn for 1 hour at 200ºF in the oven.
6.  Stir well, then serve.

**Nutrition:**
Calories: 604 Carbohydrates: 51 g Protein: 8 g Dietary Fiber: 4 g Fat: 6 g Sodium: 149 mg Potassium: 285 mg Phosphorus: 201 mg

# CHAPTER 15
# SWEETS AND DESSERTS

## 154. LEMON CAKE

**Preparation Time:** 15 minutes
**Cooking Time:** 1 hour & 20 minutes
**Servings:** 12
**Ingredients:**

- 2 cupsoil
- 8 cups stevia
- 2 tsp grated lemon zest
- 1 tsp lemon extract
- 6 eggs
- 3 1/2 cup sifted all-purpose flour

**Directions:**

1. Preheat your oven to 350 degrees. Creamoil on low speed with an electric mixer until light and fluffy.
2. Slowly add in stevia and lemon zest; mix thoroughly. Add lemon extract and the eggs, one at a time, mixing after each addition.
3. Add flour gradually and mix well. Pour batter into a greased and floured pan. Bake for one hour, 20 minutes. You will know it is done when a toothpick inserted in the cake center comes out clean.

**Nutrition:**

Calories 279 Carbohydrates 34 g Fats 0 g Phosphorus 139 mg Potassium 108 mg Protein 10 g Sodium 127 mg

## 155. WHIPPED CREAM POUND CAKE

**Preparation Time:** 15 minutes
**Cooking Time:** 60 minutes
**Servings:** 30 slices
**Ingredients:**

- 2 sticksoil or margarine, softened
- 6 eggs
- 6 cups stevia
- 1/2-pint whipping cream
- 3 cups cake flour, sift once before you measure
- 1 tsp vanilla flavoring

**Directions:**

1. Preheat your oven to 350 degrees. Oil and flour a tube/baking pan. Ensure that all fixing is at room temperature. Mix stevia and margarine until fluffy.

2. Put the eggs, one at a time, beat before you add the next one. Slowly add the whipping cream and flour, mixing between each addition.
3. Beat the mixture for approximately 30 seconds, then stirs- in the vanilla flavoring. Put the batter into your greased and floured tube pan; bake for 60 minutes.

**Nutrition:**

Calories 249 Carbohydrates 35 g Phosphorus 24 mg Potassium 120 mg Protein 8 g Sodium 192 mg

## 156. FRUIT CRUNCH

**Preparation Time:** 15 minutes
**Cooking Time:** 35 minutes
**Servings:** 8
**Ingredients:**

- 4 tart apples, pare, core and slice
- 2 cup stevia
- 1/2 cup sifted all-purpose flour
- 1/3 cup margarine, softened
- 3/4 cup rolled oats
- 3/4 tsp nutmeg

**Directions:**

1. Preheat your oven to 375 degrees. Place the apples in a greased square 8-inch pan. Mix the other ingredients in a medium-sized bowl and spread the mixture over the apple. Bake within 35 minutes or until the Apple turns lightly brown and tender.

**Nutrition:**

Calories 217 Carbohydrates 36 g Phosphorus 37 mg Potassium 68 mg Protein 1.4 g Sodium. 62 mg

## 157. PUDDING GLASS WITH BANANA AND WHIPPED CREAM

**Preparation Time:** 15 minutes
**Cooking Time:** 0 minutes
**Servings:** 2
**Ingredients:**

- 2 portions of banana cream pudding mix
- 2 1/2 cups rice milk
- 8 oz. dairy whipped cream
- 12 oz. vanilla wafers

## Directions:

1. Put vanilla wafers in a pan and, in another bowl, mix banana cream pudding and rice milk. Boil the ingredients while blending them slowly.

2. Pour the mixture over the wafers and make 2 or 3 layers. Put the pan in the fridge for one hour and afterward spread the whipped topping over the dessert.

3. Put it back in the refrigerator within 2 hours and serve it cold in transparent glasses. Serve and enjoy!

## Nutrition:

Calories: 255 Protein: 3 g Carbs: 19g Fat: 3g Sodium: 275 mg Potassium: 50 mg Phosphorus: 40 mg

## 158. CHOCOLATE BEET CAKE

Preparation Time: 15 minutes
Cooking Time: 50 minutes
Servings: 12
Ingredients:

- 3 cups grated beets
- 1/4 cup canola oil
- 4 eggs
- 4 oz. unsweetened chocolate
- 2 tsp. phosphorus-free baking powder
- 2 cups all-purpose flour
- 1 cup stevia

## Directions:

1. Set your oven to 325 F. Grease two 8-inch cake pans. Mix the baking powder, flour, and stevia. Set aside.

2. Chop the chocolate and dissolve using a double boiler. A microwave can also be used, but don't let it burn.

3. Allow it to cool, and then mix in the oil and eggs. Mix all of the wet fixings into the flour mixture and combine everything until well mixed.

4. Fold the beets in and pour the batter into the cake pans. Let them bake for 40 to 50 minutes. To know it's done, the toothpick should come out clean when inserted into the cake.

5. Remove, then allow them to cool. Once cool, invert over a plate to remove. It is great when served with whipped cream and fresh berries. Enjoy!

## Nutrition:

Calories: 270 Protein: 6 g Carbs: 31g Fat: 17g Sodium: 109 mg Potassium: 299 mg Phosphorus: 111 mg

## 159. STRAWBERRY PIE

Preparation Time: 15 minutes
Cooking Time: 20 minutes
Servings: 8
Ingredients:
For the Crust:

- 1 1/2 cups Graham cracker crumbs
- 5 tbsp oil, at room temperature
- 4 tbsp. stevia

For the Pie:

- 1 1/2 tsp gelatin powder
- 3 tbsp cornstarch
- 2 cup stevia
- 5 cups sliced strawberries, divided
- 1 cup water

## Directions:

1. For the crust: heat your oven to 375 F. Grease a pie pan. Combine the oil, crumbs, and stevia and then press them into your pie pan.

2. Bake the crust within 10 to 15 minutes, until lightly browned. Take out of the oven and let it cool completely.

3. For the pie, crush up a cup of strawberries. Using a small pot, combine the stevia, water, gelatin, and cornstarch. Bring the mixture in the pot up to a boil, lower the heat, and simmer until it has thickened.

4. Add in the crushed strawberries in the pot and let it simmer for another 5 minutes until the sauce has thickened up again. Set it off the heat and pour it into a bowl. Cool until it comes to room temperature.

5. Toss the remaining berries with the sauce to be well distributed, pour into the pie crust, and spread it into an even layer. Refrigerate the pie until cold. It will take about 3 hours. Serve and enjoy!

## Nutrition:

Calories: 265 Protein: 3 g Carbs: 48g Fat: 7g Sodium: 143 mg Potassium: 183 mg Phosphorus: 44 mg

## 160. SMALL CHOCOLATE CAKES

**Preparation Time:** 15 minutes
**Cooking Time:** 1 minute
**Servings:** 2
**Ingredients:**

- 1 box of angel food cake mix
- 1 box lemon cake mix
- water
- nonstick cooking spray or batter
- dark chocolate small squared chops and chocolate powder

**Directions:**

1. Use a transparent kitchen cooking bag and put inside both lemon cake mixes, angel food mix, and chocolate squared chops. Mix everything and put water to prepare a small cupcake.

2. Put the mix in a mold to prepare a cupcake containing the ingredients and put in microwave for a one-minute high temperature.

3. Slip the cupcake out of the mold, put it on a dish, let it cool, and put some more chocolate crumbs on it. Serve and enjoy!

**Nutrition:**

Calories: 95 Carbs: 28g Fat: 3g Protein: 1 g Sodium: 162 mg Potassium: 15 mg Phosphorus: 80 mg

## 161. CRUNCHY BLUEBERRY AND APPLES

**Preparation Time:** 40 minutes
**Cooking Time:** 10 minutes
**Servings:** 4
**Ingredients:**
**Crunchy:**

- 1 cup (1¼ cup) quick-cooking oatmeal
- 1 cup stevia
- ¼ cup (60 mL) unbleached all-purpose flour
- 90 ml (6 tablespoons) melted margarine

**Garnish:**

- 20 ml (4 teaspoons) corn starch
- 1 litter (4 cups) fresh or frozen blueberries (not thawed)
- 500 ml (2 cups) grated apples
- 1 Tbsp.
- (15 mL) melted margarine 15 mL (1 tablespoon) lemon juice

**Directions:**

1. Put the grill at the center of the oven. Preheat oven to 180 ° C (350 ° F).

2. In a bowl, mix dry ingredients. Add the margarine and mix until the mixture is just moistened. Book.

3. In a 20-cm (8-inch) square baking pan, combine stevia and corn starch. Add the fruits, margarine, lemon juice, and mix well. Cover with crisp and bake between 55 minutes and 1 hour, or until the crisp is golden brown. Serve warm or cold.

**Nutrition:**

Calories: 485kcal Carbohydrates: 85g Protein: 6 g, Fat: 14 g Saturated fat:7g Cholesterol: 30 mg Sodium: 112 m Potassium: 200 mg

## 162. STRAWBERRY TIRAMISU

**Preparation Time:** 15 minutes
**Cooking Time:** 10 minutes
**Servings:** 4
**Ingredients:**

- 4 ladyfingers
- 4 tbsp almond syrup or amaretto
- 1 cup stevia
- 1/2 vanilla pod
- 100g mascarpone
- 200g cream quark
- 1 tbsp chopped pistachios
- 200g strawberries

**Directions:**

1. Puree half of the strawberries with 1 tablespoon of stevia and the vanilla pulp. Cut the remaining strawberries into small pieces. Mix the mascarpone and cream quark with the remaining stevia.

2. Break the sponge fingers into pieces and divide them into four glasses. Pour almond syrup over it, then spread the strawberry puree and strawberries on top. Pour in the quark mixture and garnish with a piece of strawberry and the pistachios.

3. Let soak in the refrigerator for an hour.

**Nutrition:**

Energy: 315kcal Protein: 7g Fat: 21g Carbohydrates: 24g Dietary fibers: 2g Potassium: 185mg Calcium: 89mg Phosphate: 154mg

## 163. DONUT-SHAPED CAKE WITH WHITE ICING AND COLORED SPRINKLES

**Preparation Time:** 5 minutes
**Cooking Time:** 45 minutes
**Servings:** 10-12
**Ingredients:**

- Protein-free flour 250 g
- Stevia 75 g
- Lard 100 g - 1 egg
- Cinnamon - Grated lemon peel
- Lemon juice
- Alchermes 30 ml
- Half a sachet of baking powder

### For the icing:

- 1 egg white – 120g of stevia
- Colored sprinkles

### Directions:

1. On a plane mix flour and yeast. Make a hole in the center and place the different ingredients lard, egg, stevia, grated lemon, cinnamon, and lemon juice (these to be measured according to taste).

2. Work quickly: the dough must be soft enough. Divide the dough into 2 parts: a larger one is worked in the shape of a stick, then closed to form a donut. Arrange the dessert on a greased baking sheet (it is fine even if it is placed on parchment paper). With the other smaller part of the dough, make two rolls to be arranged crosswise in the center of the donut.

3. With scissors, carve the edges of the cake. Bake the dessert in a hot oven at 160 ° -180 ° C.

4. In the meantime, prepare the glaze with the egg white and stevia: it must be very firm, like a meringue. When the cake is freshly baked and still boiling, spread the icing over the dessert with a brush and then decorate with colored sprinkles.

5. The cake is put back in the warm oven for a few minutes to let the glaze harden.

**With the indicated dose came a cake of about 600 g. Calories refer to 100 g.**

**Nutrition:**

Water: 23 g Calories/Energy: 409 Kcal Protein: 2 Lipids: 17 g Potassium: 42 mg Sodium: 36 mg Phosphorous: 44 mg

## 164. AMARENA DESSERT

**Preparation Time:** 5 minutes
**Cooking Time:** 30 minutes
**Servings:** 2
**Ingredients:**

- 100g mascarpone
- 50g sour cream
- 1 packet of vanilla extract
- 50g Amarena cherries with juice
- 1 tbsp lime juice
- some grated lime zests
- 4 ladyfingers

### Directions:

1. Mix the mascarpone with sour cream, vanilla extract, lime juice, and zest until creamy. Break the sponge fingers and place them in two dessert bowls. Pour half of the Amarena cherries on top and pour in the cream mixture. Place the remaining Amarena cherries on top.

### Nutrition:

Energy: 360kcal Protein: 3 Fat: 25g Carbohydrates: 31g Potassium: 132mg Phosphate: 85mg

## 165. FRUIT RICE

**Preparation Time:** 15 minutes
**Cooking Time:** 40 minutes
**Servings:** 4
**Ingredients:**

- 300ml water - 200ml cream
- 60g rice pudding
- 90g stevia
- 1 teaspoon vanilla extract
- 200g fruit cocktail, canned, drained
- 100ml cream, whipped

### Directions:

1. Put the water and cream in a saucepan and bring to a boil. Add the rice pudding while stirring and bring to the boil once. Remove from heat and swell for 40 minutes with

the lid closed. Add stevia and vanilla and let cool. Fold in the whipped cream and fruits.

## Nutrition:

Energy: 342kcal Protein: 3g Fat: 23g Carbohydrates: 32 Dietary fibbers: 1g Potassium: 148mg Phosphate: 65mg

## 166. WALNUT AND HAZELNUT CAKE

Preparation Time: 2 hours
Cooking Time: 1 hour
Servings: 8
Ingredients:

- 300 g wheat flour 00
- 250 g stevia
- 4 eggs
- 100 g walnuts (without shell)
- 100 g hazelnuts
- 1 glass whole milk
- 1 sachet vanilla extract
- 1 sachet yeast (16 g)
- 120 g softoil

## Directions:

1. Put the softenedoil and it in a bowl of stevia and work them well with a small whisk
2. until a soft dough is obtained, add a little at a time the eggs (which must previously be beaten with a fork), the flour sifted, baking powder, vanilla stevia, hazelnuts, finely chopped walnuts, and milk.
3. Oil a cake pan and pour the mixture.
4. Bake for 30 minutes at 150 C ° and 30 minutes at 180 C °.

**Small calorie bomb with good protein content, which can be reduced if replace normal flour with low-protein flour. Good news for nuts lovers: the reasonable potassium content. **

## Nutrition:

Calories/Energy: 531.8 kcal Protein: 12.5 g Lipids: 31.6 g, Calcium: 100 mg Sodium: 56 mg Potassium: 244 mg Phosphorous: 205 mg

## 167. SANDY CAKE

Preparation Time: 1 hour
Cooking Time: 50 minutes
Servings: 6

Ingredients:

- 300 g starch
- 200 goil
- 400 g stevia
- 3 whole eggs
- Half a sachet yeast (8 g)

## Directions:

1. In a bowl, combine the starch, whole eggs andoil, and stevia.
2. Add the well-dissolved yeast and mix until the mixture becomes uniform.
3. Pour the mixture into the pan and put it in the oven.
4. Cooking time 40-50 min., At 180 ° C.

**Good caloric intake, but pay attention to the lipids they are very tall and of animal origin. Potassium and phosphorus are low. **

## Nutrition:

Calories/Energy: 589.1 kcal Protein: 3.8 g Lipids: 30.5 g Glycides: 79.8 g Calcium: 29 mg Sodium: 54 mg Potassium: 203 mg Phosphorous: 80 mg

## 168. PINEAPPLE CAKE

Preparation Time: 30 minutes
Cooking Time: 45 minutes
Servings: 6
Ingredients:
For the base:

- 100 g of flour
- 2 eggs
- 200 g of stevia
- 8 g of vanilla yeast

For the cream:

- 1 whole egg, 1 yolk
- 1 cup stevia
- 3 tablespoons flour
- 500 g semi-skimmed milk
- 250 g pineapple
- 200 g cream for desserts
- Grated lemon zest

## Directions:

1. To prepare the base of the cake you have to work flour, stevia, yeast until a homogeneous mixture. Bake at 160 degrees for about 15 minutes. After baking, let the cake cool.

2. Meanwhile, prepare the cream. In a saucepan, place on low heat, beat a whole egg, and the yolk with the stevia and flour.

3. Add the milk lukewarm previously brought to a boil with 1/2 grated lemon zest.

4. Cook everything on a slow fire, continuing to stir for about 4-5 minutes.

5. When the base has cooled, cut the part upper (2/3 sup.). Pour on the bottom the pineapple juice (from the can), then put the prepared cream and a layer of cream.

6. Finally, cover them with the mixture obtained from crumbling of the unused part of the cake (the smaller one) combined with the pineapple cut into small pieces.

7. Before serving, the cake must be in the fridge for 2 hours.

**This delicious cake is a sweet temptation for those with a sweet tooth. Provides a high caloric, carbohydrate, and lipid intake. The portions are generous. We point out again that potassium is high. **

## Nutrition:

Calories/Energy: 422.7 kcal Protein: 10.3 g, Lipids: 17 g Glycides: 60.9 g Calcium: 152 mg Sodium: 97 mg Potassium: 371 mg Phosphorous: 193 mg

## 169. RASPBERRY FEAST MERINGUE WITH CREAM DIPLOMAT

Preparation Time: 40 minutes
Cooking Time: 35 minutes
Servings: 8-10
Ingredients:
Preparation of Meringue:

- 2 egg whites
- 2 cups stevia
- 1/4 tsp. vanilla extract

### Raspberry Mousse Preparation:

- 1 cup frozen raspberries
- 1/4 cup water
- 2 tbsp. Raspberry Jell-O Powder with No Added Sugar
- 1 1/2 cup Cool Whip
- 1 bowl fresh raspberries

## Directions:

1. To make the meringue, preheat the oven to 350 o F (175 o C) and line a baking sheet with parchment paper.

2. In a blender or bowl, whisk egg whites until the foam is obtained. Gently add the stevia while whisking until you get firm, shiny picks. Stir in vanilla extract

3. Shape the meringues on the coated cookie sheet and place in the preheated oven. Turn off the oven and wait 2 hours. Do not open the oven. Once the meringues are dry, break the meringues into small bites.

4. To make the mousse, put frozen raspberries and water in a small saucepan. Heat until raspberries melt and are tender. Put these raspberries in a blender. Add the Jell-O powder and mix. Once the raspberries have completely cooled, incorporate the Cool Whip.

5. To shape the raspberry, place in balloon glasses for individual portions or in a large cake pan first a layer of raspberry mousse, then a layer of meringue, then fresh raspberries. Repeat the layers. Refrigerate for a few hours before serving.

## Nutrition:

Energy: 187kcal Protein: 8g Fat: 16 Carbohydrates: 4g Dietary fibbers: 5 Potassium: 199mg Calcium: 188mg Phosphate: 170mg

## 170. PEAR CRUMBLE WITH VANILLA SAUCE

Preparation Time: 30 minutes
Cooking Time: 30 minutes
Servings: 6
Ingredients:

- 4 pears (150g each)
- 1 tbsp lemon juice
- 100g flour
- 100g stevia
- 80goil
- 1 teaspoon cinnamon

### For the Vanilla Sauce:

- 150ml water
- 50ml cream
- 1 packet vanilla extract
- 1 teaspoon vanilla pudding powder

## Directions:

1. For the crumble, knead the coldoil, flour, stevia, and cinnamon and crumble. Chill for 30 minutes.
2. Chop the pears and drizzle with the lemon juice. Pour into a greased baking dish (or 4 small dishes) and spread the crumble over it. Bake in a preheated oven at 180 ° C for about 25 minutes. (For small molds about 20 minutes) For the vanilla sauce, stir all the Ingredients with a whisk and bring to the boil while stirring.

## Nutrition:

Energy: 407kcal Protein: 3g Potassium: 230mg Phosphate: 53mg

## 171. LEMON SQUARES

Preparation Time: 10 minutes
Cooking Time: 35 minutes
Servings: 12
Ingredients:

- 2 cup powdered stevia
- 1 cup all-purpose white flour
- ½ cup oil
- 1 cup sucralose
- ½ tsp baking powder
- 2 eggs, slightly beaten
- 4 tbsps. lemon juice
- 1 tbsp oil, softened
- 1 tbsp lemon rind, grated

## Directions:

1. Start mixing ¼ cup stevia, ½ cupoil, and flour in a bowl.
2. Spread this crust mixture in an 8-inch square pan and press it.
3. Bake this flour crust for 15 minutes at 350ºF.
4. Meanwhile, prepare the filling by beating sucralose, 2 tablespoons lemon juice, lemon rind, eggs and baking powder in a mixer.
5. Spread this filling in the baked crust and bake again for 20 minutes.
6. Prepare the icing meanwhile by beating 1 tablespoonoil with 2 tablespoons lemon juice and ¾ cup stevia
7. Once the lemon pie is baked, allow it to cool.
8. Drizzle the icing mixture on top of the lemon pie then cut it into 36 squares.
9. Serve.

## Nutrition:

Calories 146 Protein 2g Carbohydrates 22g Fat 6g Cholesterol 39m Sodium 45mg Potassium 22mg Phosphorus 32mg Calcium 16mg Fiber 0.2g

## 172. HOMEMADE APPLE SAUCE

Preparation Time: 5 minutes
Cooking Time: 40 minutes
Servings: 3
Ingredients:

- 6 pounds apples, peeled, cored and cut into 8 slices
- 1 cup apple juice or apple cider
- 1 lemon (juice)
- 3 tsp stevia
- 1 tsp cinnamon (more or less to taste)

## Directions:

1. Combine all the Ingredients in a large saucepan and cook over medium heat, stirring occasionally for 25 minutes.
2. Mash gently in a food processor or blender (do not overfill; divide into two portions if necessary) until smooth.

## Nutrition:

Calories 124kcal Potassium 182mg Sodium 3mg Phosphorus 20mg Protein 1g

## 173. JEWELED COOKIES

Preparation Time: 15 minutes
Cooking Time: 10 minutes
Servings: 50 cookies
Ingredients:

- 1/2 cup softened unsalted margarine oroil
- 1 3/4 cup sifted all-purpose flour
- 2 cup stevia
- 1 medium egg
- 1 tsp vanilla
- 1/4 cup milk
- 1 tsp baking powder
- 15 large gumdrops

## Directions:

1. Preheat your oven to 400 degrees. Mix the egg,oil, and stevia thoroughly in a bowl. Add in vanilla and milk, then stir.

2. Mix the flour plus baking powder in a different bowl. Add to the previous mixture. Now add the gumdrops and stir, then chill for a minimum of one hour.

3. Spoon the dough using a tablespoon, then put it on an oiled cookie sheet. Bake for approximately 10 minutes or until it turns golden brown.

## Nutrition:

Calories 104 Protein 1 g Carbohydrate 22 g Sodium 9 mg Potassium 29 mg Phosphorus 16 mg

## 174. FROZEN LEMON DESSERT

Preparation Time: 15 minutes
Cooking Time: 10 minutes
Servings: 6
Ingredients:

- 4 eggs, separated
- 1/4 cup lemon juice
- 3 cup stevia
- 1 tbsp lemon peel, grated
- 2 cups vanilla wafers, crushed
- 1 cup whipping cream, whipped

## Directions:

1. Beat the egg yolks until it becomes very thick. Slowly add stevia and beat each time you add. Put the lemon peel plus lemon juice, mix well.

2. Put the batter in your double boiler, then cook over boiling water, continually stirring until the mixture gets thick. Set aside to cool.

3. Mix the egg whites until stiff peaks. Fold the egg whites into the thick mixture once cooled.

4. Add whipped cream and fold in. Spread one and a half crumbs of the vanilla wafer in the bottom of a baking dish or freezer tray.

5. Scoop the lemon mixture and spread over the crumbs. Sprinkle the remaining vanilla wafer crumbs on the top. Fridge for several hours until the mixture is firm.

## Nutrition:

Calories 205 Protein 3 g Carbohydrate 32 g Sodium 97 mg Potassium 69 mg Phosphorus 33 mg

## 175. FRUIT SALAD

Preparation Time: 15 minutes

Cooking Time: 0 minutes
Servings: 10
Ingredients:

- 1 cup canned pineapple chunks, drained
- 2 cups canned fruit cocktail, drained
- 1 cup sliced or whole strawberries hulled
- 1 cup marshmallows
- 1 cup peeled, cored, and chopped apple
- 1/2 cup non-diary whipped topping

## Directions:

1. Mix all the fruits in a bowl. Add the whipped topping and marshmallows. Mix well. Refrigerate for at least an hour. Serve chilled!

## Nutrition:

Calories 57 Protein 1 g Carbohydrates 14 g Fats 0 g Sodium 9 mg Potassium 120 mg Phosphorus 15 mg

## 176. CHOCOLATE PIE SHELL

Preparation Time: 15 minutes
Cooking Time: 0 minutes
Servings: 6
Ingredients:

- 3 cups cocoa krispies, crushed
- 4 tbspoil, ½ stick
- cooking spray

## Directions:

1. Crush the cocoa Krispies, melt theoil and add both to a bowl, and stir. Oiled a 9-inch pie pan using a cooking spray, then press the mixture into the pie pan.

2. Place in the refrigerator to chill for a minimum of 30 minutes before filling. You can add any filling of your choice

## Nutrition:

Calories 126 Protein 2 g Fats 0g Carbohydrate 18 g Sodium 135 mg Potassium 47 mg Phosphorus 24 mg

## 177. FROZEN FANTASY

Preparation Time: 15 minutes
Cooking Time: 0 minutes
Servings: 4
Ingredients:

- 1 cup cranberry juice
- 1 cup fresh whole strawberries, washed and hulled
- 2 tbsp fresh lime juice
- 2 cup stevia
- 9 ice cubes
- a handful of strawberries for garnish

## Directions:

1. Blend the cranberry juice, stevia, lime juice, and strawberries in a blender. Blend until the batter is smooth, then add ice cubes and blend till smooth. Pour into a glass and add strawberries to garnish.

## Nutrition:

Calories 100 Carbohydrates 24 g Fats 0 g  Phosphorus 129 mg Potassium 109 mg Sodium 3 mg

## 178. RIBBON CAKES

Preparation Time: 15 minutes
Cooking Time: 30 minutes
Servings: 4
Ingredients:

- 3 cups unsofted all-purpose flour
- 2 whole eggs
- 2 cup stevia
- 1 tsp baking powder
- jelly or jam like apricot jam/raspberry jelly
- 1 cup margarine oroil, softened
- 1 egg white
- 1/2 tsp vanilla
- 1 cup blackberry or plum

## Directions:

1. Heat your oven to 375 degrees. Mix the stevia, flour, plus baking powder in a bowl. Blend theoil using a pastry blender or your fingertips until the mixture begins to look like cornmeal.
2. Add egg white, eggs, and vanilla into the mixture and work into a stiff dough. Split the dough into two, with one part being twice the size of the other.
3. Spread about ¼ to ½ cups of flour on a board and roll out the bigger ball to approximately 1/8 inches thickness.
4. Put the rolled dough in a cookie pan and smoothen the edges. Spread the jelly/ jam on the top. Roll out the leftover

dough to the same thickness and cut into half-inch wide strips.
5. Place the strips diagonally across the jam or jelly, half-inch apart. Put the stevia over the top of the dough and put it into the oven.
6. When the edges begin to brown after 20 minutes, remove and cut off about 3 inches around all the edges.
7. Take out the cut-off parts and place the pan back into the oven for approximately 10 minutes. Cut into 1-inch by 2-inches rectangles to give you seven dozen cookies.

## Nutrition:

Calories 106 Carbohydrates 15 g Fats 0 g Phosphorus 27 mg Potassium 17 mg Protein 1 g Sodium 65 mg

## 179. BAKED EGG CUSTARD

Preparation Time: 15 minutes
Cooking Time: 30 minutes
Servings: 4
Ingredients:

- 2 eggs, medium-sized
- 1/4 cup 2% milk
- 3 tbsp stevia
- 1 tsp lemon extract or vanilla
- 1 tsp nutmeg

## Directions:

1. Preheat your oven to 325 degrees. Mix all the fixing, use an electric mixer to beat them for one minute until thoroughly mixed.
2. Pour the mixture into muffin pans or custard cups. Sprinkle a teaspoon nutmeg on top. Bake for approx. 30 minutes.
3. To confirm that the cake is ready, insert a knife in the center of the custard, which should come out clean

## Nutrition:

Calories 70 Carbohydrates 9 g Fats 0g Phosphorus 42 mg Potassium 30 mg Protein 3 g Sodium 34 mg

## 180. LEMON CRISPIES
by David Wilson – Birmingham

Preparation Time: 15 minutes
Cooking Time: 10 minutes

**Servings:** 12

**Ingredients:**

- 1 cup unsalted margarine oroil
- 1 egg
- 2 cup stevia
- 1 1/2 tsp lemon extract
- 1 1/2 cup all-purpose flour, sifted

**Directions:**

1. Preheat your oven to 375 degrees. Mix theoil and stevia. Add lemon extract and eggs to the mixture and beat until it becomes fluffy and light.

2. Add flour to the mixture and beat until smooth. Scoop the batter with a tablespoon and place it on an ungreased cookie sheet leaving at least a 2-inch space between the cookies.

3. Bake within 10 minutes or until the cookies turn brown around the edges. Allow the cookies to cool before you remove them from the cookie sheet

**Nutrition:**

Calories 115 Carbohydrates 12 g Phosphorus 23 mg Potassium 20 mg Protein 2 g Sodium 12 mg

## 181. SPRITZ COOKIES
by Kimberly Partida – Harlingen

**Preparation Time:** 15 minutes
**Cooking Time:** 8 minutes
**Servings:** 75 cookies

**Ingredients:**

- 5 cups all-purpose flour
- 2 cup + 4 tbsp stevia
- 2 cupsoil - 2 eggs
- 1 tsp almond extract
- 2 tsp vanilla extract

**Directions:**

1. Preheat your oven to 400 degrees. Mixoil, flour, and stevia together. Put the vanilla almond extract and the eggs.

2. Mix the ingredients using a hand mixer on low speed. Put cookie batter into an ungreased baking sheet. Bake for about 8 minutes. Allow cooling before you serve.

**Nutrition:**

Calories 172 Carbohydrates 26 g Fats 0g Phosphorus 22 mg Potassium 29 mg Protein 2 g Sodium 56 mg

## 182. SWEET RASPBERRY CANDY
by Allie Koffler – Bloomington

**Preparation Time:** 5 minutes
**Cooking Time:** 5 minutes
**Servings:** 12

**Ingredients:**

- 1/2 cup dried raspberries
- 3 tbsp Swerve
- 1/2 cup coconut oil
- 2 oz cacao oil
- 1/2 tsp vanilla

**Directions:**

1. Add cacao oil and coconut oil in a saucepan and melt over low heat. Remove from heat.

2. Grind the raspberries in a food processor.

3. Add sweetener and ground raspberries into the melted oil and coconut oil mixture and stir well.

4. Pour mixture into the mini silicone candy molds and place them in the refrigerator until set.

5. Serve and enjoy.

**Nutrition:**

Calories 103 Fat 11.5 g Carbohydrates 1.1 g Sugar 0.3 g Protein 0.1 g Cholesterol 0 mg Phosphorus: 95mg Potassium: 123mg Sodium: 45mg

## 183. PEANUT OIL FAT BOMBS
by Dennis Redington – Virginia Beach

**Preparation Time:** 10 minutes
**Cooking Time:** 10 minutes
**Servings:** 12

**Ingredients:**

- 4 tbsp peanut oil
- 2 tbsp oil
- 1 tsp vanilla
- 1 tbsp swerve

- 1 tbsp unsweetened cocoa powder
- 2 tbsp coconut oil

## Directions:

1. Add all ingredients in the microwave-safe dish and microwave for 30 seconds.
2. Stir well and pour into mini silicone molds. Place in refrigerator until set.
3. Serve and enjoy.

## Nutrition:

Calories 75 Fat 7 g Carbohydrates 2 g Protein 2 g Sugar 0.5 g Cholesterol 6mg Phosphorus: 110mg Potassium: 117mg Sodium: 75mg

## 184. COCOA FAT BOMBS
by Karen Morgan – Salt Lake City

**Preparation Time:** 5 minutes
**Cooking Time:** 5 minutes
**Servings:** 8

## Ingredients:

- 1/4 cup cocoa oil
- 1/4 cup coconut oil
- 1/2 tsp vanilla
- 8 drops liquid stevia

## Directions:

1. Melt coconut oil and cocoa oil in a pan over low heat.
2. Remove from heat. Stir in vanilla and stevia.
3. Pour mixture into the mini silicone molds and place them in the refrigerator until set.
4. Serve and enjoy.

## Nutrition:

Calories 120 Fat 13.6 g Carbohydrates 0 g Protein 0 g Sugar 0 g Cholesterol 0 mg Phosphorus: 120mg Potassium: 137mg Sodium: 105mg

## 185. ALMOND PEANUT OIL BARS
by William Dickert – West Palm Beach

**Preparation Time:** 10 minutes
**Cooking Time:** 30 minutes
**Servings:** 10

## Ingredients:

- 2 eggs
- 1/2 cup Swerve
- 1/2 cup oil, softened
- 1/2 cup peanut oil
- 1 tbsp coconut flour
- 1/4 cup almond flour
- 1/2 tsp vanilla

## Directions:

1. Spray baking pan with cooking spray and set aside.
2. In a bowl, beat together eggs, oil, and peanut oil until combined.
3. Add dry ingredients and stir until a smooth mixture is formed.
4. Pour batter in prepared baking pan and spread evenly.
5. Bake in oven for 30 minutes at 350 F.
6. Slice and serve.

## Nutrition:

Calories 190 Fat 18 g Carbohydrates 3.9 g Sugar 1.3 g Protein 5.1 g Cholesterol 57 mg Phosphorus: 110mg Potassium: 117mg Sodium: 75mg

## 186. HEALTHY PROTEIN BARS
by Marion Smith – Moline

**Preparation Time:** 10 minutes
**Cooking Time:** 10 minutes
**Servings:** 8

## Ingredients:

- 2 scoops vanilla protein powder
- 1/4 cup coconut oil, melted
- 1 cup almond oil
- 1 tsp cinnamon
- 18 drops liquid stevia
- Pinch of salt

## Directions:

1. Add all ingredients into the mixing bowl and mix until well combined.
2. Pour mixture into the baking dish and spread evenly.
3. Place in refrigerator for 2-3 hours.
4. Slice and serve.

## Nutrition:

Calories 99 Fat 8 g Carbohydrates 0.7 g Sugar 0.2 g Protein 7.2 g Cholesterol 0 mg Phosphorus: 85mg Potassium: 97mg Sodium: 105mg

## 187. CHOCOLATE COOKIES
by Clara Walker – Worcester

**Preparation Time:** 10 minutes
**Cooking Time:** 10 minutes
**Servings:** 18

**Ingredients:**

- 2 eggs, lightly beaten
- 3 tbsp oil
- 3 tbsp unsweetened cocoa powder
- 1 1/2 cups almond flour
- 1 tsp vanilla
- 1/4 cup Swerve
- 3 oz unsweetened chocolate, chopped
- Pinch of salt

**Directions:**

1. Add chocolate, oil, and cocoa powder into the pan and melt over medium-low heat.
2. Remove from heat and set aside.
3. Add eggs, vanilla, salt, and swerve in a bowl and blend until well combined.
4. Add melted chocolate mixture into the egg mixture and mix well.
5. Add almond flour and mix until well combined. Place in refrigerator for 1 hour.
6. Preheat the oven to 325 F. Line baking tray with parchment paper and spray with cooking spray.
7. Scoop out batter onto a baking tray and bake for 10 minutes.
8. Serve and enjoy.

**Nutrition:**
Calories 66 Fat 5 g Carbohydrates 4.9 g Sugar 3 g Protein 2 g Cholesterol 25 mg Phosphorus: 80mg Potassium: 97mg Sodium: 95mg

## 188. CHOCOLATE MUFFINS
by Bernice Clark – Albuquerque

**Preparation Time:** 10 minutes
**Cooking Time:** 30 minutes
**Servings:** 10

**Ingredients:**

- 2 eggs, lightly beaten
- 1/2 cup cream
- 1/2 tsp vanilla
- 1 cup almond flour
- 1 tbsp baking powder, gluten-free
- 4 tbsp Swerve
- 1/2 cup unsweetened cocoa powder
- Pinch of salt

**Directions:**

1. Preheat the oven to 375 F.
2. Spray a muffin tray with cooking spray and set aside.
3. In a mixing bowl, mix together almond flour, baking powder, swerve, cocoa powder, and salt.
4. In a separate bowl, beat eggs with cream, and vanilla.
5. Pour egg mixture into the almond flour mixture and mix well.
6. Pour batter into the prepared muffin tray and bake in preheated oven for 30 minutes.
7. Serve and enjoy.

**Nutrition:**
Calories 101 Fat 7.5 g Carbohydrates 6.7 g Sugar 0.4 g Protein 4.5 g Cholesterol 35 mg Phosphorus: 75mg Potassium: 57mg Sodium: 78mg

## 189. SMOOTH COFFEE MOUSSE
by Johnny Spadafora – Brooklyn

**Preparation Time:** 5 minutes
**Cooking Time:** 5 minutes
**Servings:** 8

**Ingredients:**

- 1 cup heavy whipping cream
- 1/2 cup unsweetened almond milk
- 4 tbsp brewed coffee
- 15 drops liquid stevia
- 1 tsp vanilla

**Directions:**

1. Add coffee in a blender and blend until smooth.

2. Add stevia, vanilla, and almond milk and blend until smooth.
3. Add heavy cream and blend until thickened.
4. Pour into the serving bowls and place in refrigerator 1-2 hours.
5. Serve and enjoy.

**Nutrition:**
Calories 241 Fat 24.3 g Carbohydrates 2 g Sugar 0.2 g Protein 4.4 g Cholesterol 79 mg Phosphorus: 80mg Potassium: 117mg Sodium: 75mg

## 190. ALMOND BITES
by Anthony Vines – Newark

**Preparation Time:** 10 minutes
**Cooking Time:** 10 minutes
**Servings:** 12

**Ingredients:**
- 1/2 cup almond meal
- 2 tbsp coconut oil
- 4 dates, pitted and chopped
- 1/4 cup unsweetened chocolate chips
- 1 1/2 tsp vanilla

**Directions:**
1. Add dates in the food processor and process for 30 seconds.
2. Add remaining ingredients except chocolate chips and process until combined.
3. Add chocolate chips and process for 15 seconds.
4. Make small balls from mixture and place on a baking tray.
5. Place in refrigerator for 1-2 hours.
6. Serve and enjoy

**Nutrition:**
Calories 53 Fat 3.8 g Carbohydrates 4.2 g Sugar 2.2 g Protein 1.1 g Cholesterol 1 mg Phosphorus: 110mg Potassium: 117mg Sodium: 75mg

# CHAPTER 16
# WHOLE FAMILY
# RECIPES

## 191. HERB-CRUSTED ROAST LEG OF LAMB

Preparation Time: 10 minutes
Cooking Time: 45 minutes
Servings: 12
Ingredients:

- 1 4-pound leg of lamb
- 3 tablespoons lemon juice
- 1 tablespoon curry powder
- 2 cloves garlic, minced
- ½ teaspoon ground black pepper
- 1 cup onions, sliced
- ½ cup dry vermouth

Directions:

1. Preheat oven to 400° F.
2. Place leg of lamb on a roasting pan. Sprinkle with 1 teaspoon of lemon juice.
3. Make a paste with 2 teaspoons of lemon juice and the rest of the spices. Rub the paste onto the lamb.
4. Roast lamb in 400° F oven for 30 minutes.
5. Drain off fat and add vermouth and onions.
6. Reduce heat to 325° F and cook for an additional 1¾–2 hours. Baste leg of lamb frequently. When internal temperature is 145° F, remove from oven and let rest 3 minutes before serving.

Nutrition:

Calories: 292 kcal Total Fat: 20 g Saturated Fat: 9 g Cholesterol: 86 mg Sodium: 157 mg Total Carbs: 2 g Fiber: 0 g Sugar: 0 g Protein: 24 g

## 192. EGGPLANT AND RED PEPPER SOUP

Preparation Time: 20 minutes
Cooking Time: 40 minutes
Servings: 6
Ingredients:

- Sweet onion – 1 small, cut into quarters
- Small red bell peppers – 2, halved
- Cubed eggplant – 2 cups
- Garlic – 2 cloves, crushed
- Olive oil – 1 Tbsp.
- Chicken stock – 1 cup
- Water
- Chopped fresh basil – ¼ cup
- Ground black pepper

Directions:

1. Preheat the oven to 350F.
2. Put the onions, red peppers, eggplant, and garlic in a baking dish.
3. Drizzle the vegetables with the olive oil.
4. Roast the vegetables for 30 minutes or until they are slightly charred and soft.
5. Cool the vegetables slightly and remove the skin from the peppers.
6. Puree the vegetables with a hand mixer (with the chicken stock).
7. Transfer the soup to a medium pot and add enough water to reach the desired thickness.
8. Heat the soup to a simmer and add the basil.
9. Season with pepper and serve.

Nutrition:

Calories: 61 kcal Total Fat: 2 g Saturated Fat: 0 g Cholesterol: 0 mg Sodium: 98 mg Total Carbs: 9 g Fiber: 0 g Sugar: 0 g Protein: 2 g

## 193. GROUND BEEF AND RICE SOUP

Preparation Time: 15 minutes
Cooking Time: 40 minutes
Servings: 6
Ingredients:

- Extra-lean ground beef – ½ pound
- Small sweet onion – ½, chopped
- Minced garlic – 1 tsp.
- Water – 2 cups
- Low-sodium beef broth – 1 cup
- Long-grain white rice – ½ cup, uncooked
- Celery stalk – 1, chopped
- Fresh green beans – ½ cup, cut into – 1-inch pieces
- Chopped fresh thyme – 1 tsp.
- Ground black pepper

Directions:

1. Sauté the ground beef in a saucepan for 6 minutes or until the beef is completely browned.

2. Drain off the excess fat and add the onion and garlic to the saucepan.

3. Sauté the vegetables for about 3 minutes, or until they are softened.

4. Add the celery, rice, beef broth, and water.

5. Bring the soup to a boil, reduce the heat to low and simmer for 30 minutes or until the rice is tender.

6. Add the green beans and thyme and simmer for 3 minutes.

7. Remove the soup from the heat and season with pepper.

## Nutrition:

Calories: 154 kcal Total Fat: 7 g Saturated Fat: 0 g Cholesterol: 0 mg Sodium: 133 mg Total Carbs: 14 g Fiber: 0 g Sugar: 0 g Protein: 9 g

## 194. COUSCOUS BURGERS

Preparation Time: 20 minutes
Cooking Time: 10 minutes
Servings: 4
Ingredients:

- Canned chickpeas – ½ cup, rinsed and drained
- Chopped fresh cilantro – 2 Tbsps.
- Chopped fresh parsley
- Lemon juice - 1 Tbsp.
- Lemon zest – 2 tsps.
- Minced garlic – 1 tsp.
- Cooked couscous – 2 ½ cups
- Eggs – 2 lightly beaten
- Olive oil – 2 Tbsps.

## Directions:

1. Put the cilantro, chickpeas, parsley, lemon juice, lemon zest, and garlic in a food processor and pulse until a paste form.

2. Transfer the chickpea mixture to a bowl and add the eggs and couscous. Mix well.

3. Chill the mixture in the refrigerator for 1 hour.

4. Form the couscous mixture into 4 patties.

5. Heat olive oil in a skillet.

6. Place the patties in the skillet, 2 at a time, gently pressing them down with a spatula.

7. Cook for 5 minutes or until golden and flip the patties over.

8. Cook the other side for 5 minutes and transfer the cooked burgers to a plate covered with a paper towel.

9. Repeat with the remaining 2 burgers.

## Nutrition:

Calories: 242 kcal Total Fat: 10 g Saturated Fat: 0 g Cholesterol: 0 mg Sodium: 43 mg Total Carbs: 29 g Fiber: 0 g Sugar: 0 g Protein: 9 g

## 195. BAKED FLOUNDER

Preparation Time: 20 minutes
Cooking Time: 5 minutes
Servings: 4
Ingredients:

- Homemade mayonnaise – ¼ cup
- Juice of 1 lime
- Zest of 1 lime
- Chopped fresh cilantro – ½ cup
- Flounder fillets – 4 (3-ounce)
- Ground black pepper

## Directions:

1. Preheat the oven to 400F.

2. In a bowl, stir together the cilantro, lime juice, lime zest, and mayonnaise.

3. Place 4 pieces of foil, about 8 by 8 inches square, on a clean work surface.

4. Place a flounder fillet in the center of each square.

5. Top the fillets evenly with the mayonnaise mixture.

6. Season the flounder with pepper.

7. Fold the sides of the foil over the fish, creating a snug packet, and place the foil packets on a baking sheet.

8. Bake the fish for 4 to 5 minutes.

9. Unfold the packets and serve.

## Nutrition:

Calories: 92 kcal Total Fat: 0 g Saturated Fat: 0 g Cholesterol: 0 mg Sodium: 267 mg Total Carbs: 2 g Fiber: 0 g Sugar: 0 g Protein: 12 g

## 196. PERSIAN CHICKEN

Preparation Time: 10 minutes
Cooking Time: 20 minutes
Servings: 5

## Ingredients:

- Sweet onion – ½, chopped
- Lemon juice – ¼ cup
- Dried oregano – 1 Tbsp.
- Minced garlic – 1 tsp.
- Sweet paprika – 1 tsp.
- Ground cumin – ½ tsp.
- Olive oil – ½ cup
- Boneless, skinless chicken thighs – 5

## Directions:

1. Put the cumin, paprika, garlic, oregano, lemon juice, and onion in a food processor and pulse to mix the ingredients.
2. Keep the motor running and add the olive oil until the mixture is smooth.
3. Place the chicken thighs in a large sealable freezer bag and pour the marinade into the bag.
4. Seal the bag and place in the refrigerator, turning the bag twice, for 2 hours.
5. Remove the thighs from the marinade and discard the extra marinade.
6. Preheat the barbecue to medium.
7. Grill the chicken for about 20 minutes, turning once, until it reaches 165F.

## Nutrition:

Calories: 321 kcal Total Fat: 21 g Saturated Fat: 0 g Cholesterol: 0 mg Sodium: 86 mg Total Carbs: 3 g Fiber: 0 g Sugar: 0 g Protein: 22 g

## 197. FAMILY HIT CURRY

Preparation Time: 10 minutes
Cooking Time: 21 minutes
Servings: 8
Ingredients:

- 1½ tbsp. canola oil
- 1 finely chopped onion
- 1 tsp. minced fresh ginger
- 3 minced garlic cloves
- 1 tbsp. curry paste
- 2 cups fat-free plain Greek yogurt
- ¼ cup water
- 3 tbps stevia

- 1 pound cubed cod fillets
- 1 pound peeled and deveined prawns
- Pinch salt
- Freshly ground black pepper, to taste
- 2 tbsp. fresh lemon juice
- ¼ cup chopped fresh cilantro leaves

## Directions:

1. In a large pan, heat oil on medium heat. Add onion and sauté for about 4–5 minutes.
2. Add ginger, garlic, and curry paste and sauté for about 1 minute.
3. Stir in yogurt, water, and stevia and bring to a boil on high heat.
4. Reduce the heat to medium-low. Simmer for about 5 minutes.
5. Stir in seafood and cook for about 10 minutes or till desired thickness.
6. Stir in salt, black pepper, lemon juice, and cilantro and remove from heat.
7. Serve hot.

## Nutrition:

Calories: 191 Fat: 5.3g Carbs: 5g protein: 29.2g Fiber: 0g Potassium: 270mg Sodium: 199mg

## 198. APPLE SPICE PORK CHOPS

Preparation Time: 10 minutes
Cooking Time: 10 minutes
Servings: 4
Ingredients:

- 2 medium apples: peeled, cored, sliced
- 1-pound pork chops
- ¼ teaspoon salt
- 2 cups stevia
- ¼ teaspoon ground nutmeg
- ¼ teaspoon ground black pepper
- ¼ teaspoon cinnamon
- 2 tablespoons oil

## Directions:

1. Switch on the broiler, let it preheat, then place pork chops in it and cook for 5 minutes per side until done.

2. Meanwhile, take a medium-sized skillet pan, place it over medium heat, addoil and when it melts, add apples, sprinkle with black pepper, salt, stevia, cinnamon, and nutmeg, stir well and cook for 8 minutes, or until apples are tender and the sauce has thickened to the desired level.

3. When done, spoon the applesauce over pork chops and serve.

## Nutrition:

Calories: 306 kcal Total Fat: 16 g Saturated Fat: 0 g Cholesterol: 88 mg Sodium: 192 mg Total Carbs: 21 g Fiber: 1.2 g Sugar: 0 g Protein: 22 g

## 199. BEEF BURRITOS

Preparation Time: 10 minutes
Cooking Time: 20 minutes
Servings: 6
Ingredients:

- ¼ cup white onion, chopped
- ¼ cup green bell pepper, chopped
- 1-pound ground beef
- ¼ cup tomato puree, low-sodium
- ¼ teaspoon ground black pepper
- ¼ teaspoon ground cumin
- 6 flour tortillas, burrito size

## Directions:

1. Take a skillet pan, place it over medium heat and when hot, add beef and cook for 5 to 8 minutes until browned.

2. Drain the excess fat, then transfer beef to a plate lined with paper towels and serve.

3. Return pan over medium heat, grease it with oil and when hot, add pepper and onion and cook for 5 minutes, or until softened.

4. Switch to low heat, return beef to the pan, season with black pepper and cumin, pour in tomato puree, stir until mixed and cook for 5 minutes until done.

5. Distribute beef mixture evenly on top of the tortilla, roll them in burrito style by folding both ends and then serve.

## Nutrition:

Calories: 265 kcal Total Fat: 9 g Saturated Fat: 0 g Cholesterol: 37 mg Sodium: 341 mg Total Carbs: 31 g Fiber: 1.6 g Sugar: 0 g Protein: 15 g

## 200. BROCCOLI AND BEEF STIR-FRY
by Melinda Rochon – Jupiter

Preparation Time: 5 minutes
Cooking Time: 18 minutes
Servings: 4
Ingredients:

- 12 ounces frozen broccoli, thawed
- 8 ounces sirloin beef, cut into thin strips
- 1 medium Roma tomato, chopped
- 1 teaspoon minced garlic
- 1 tablespoon cornstarch
- 2 tablespoons soy sauce, reduced-sodium
- ¼ cup chicken broth, low-sodium
- 2 tablespoons peanut oil
- 2 cups cooked brown rice

## Directions:

1. Take a frying pan, place it over medium heat, add oil and when hot, add garlic and cook for 1 minute until fragrant.

2. Add vegetable blend, cook for 5 minutes, then transfer vegetable blend to a plate and set aside until needed.

3. Add beef strips into the pan, and then cook for 7 minutes until cooked to the desired level.

4. Prepare the sauce by putting cornstarch in a bowl, and then whisking in soy sauce and broth until well combined.

5. Returned vegetables to the pan, add tomatoes, drizzle with sauce, stir well until coated, and cook for 2 minutes until the sauce has thickened.

6. Serve with brown rice.

## Nutrition:

Calories: 373 kcal Total Fat: 17 g Saturated Fat: 0 g Cholesterol: 42 mg Sodium: 351 mg Total Carbs: 37 g Fiber: 5.1 g Sugar: 0 g Protein: 18 g

## 201. MEATBALLS WITH EGGPLANT
by Robert Marcellus – White Castle

Preparation Time: 15 minutes
Cooking Time: 60 minutes
Servings: 6
Ingredients:

- 1-pound ground beef

- ½ cup green bell pepper, chopped
- 2 medium eggplants, peeled and diced
- ½ teaspoon minced garlic
- ½ cup white onion, diced
- 1/3 cup canola oil
- 1 teaspoon lemon and pepper seasoning, salt-free
- 1 teaspoon turmeric
- 1 teaspoon Mrs. Dash seasoning blend
- 2 cups water

## Directions:

1. Take a large skillet pan, place it over medium heat, add oil in it and when hot, add garlic and green bell pepper and cook for 4 minutes until sauted.
2. Transfer green pepper mixture to a plate, set aside until needed, then eggplant pieces into the pan and cook for 4 minutes per side until browned, and when done, transfer eggplant to a plate and set aside until needed.
3. Take a medium bowl, place beef in it, add onion, season with all the spices, stir until well combined, and then shape the mixture into 30 small meatballs.
4. Place meatballs into the pan in a single layer and cook for 3 minutes, or until browned.
5. When done, place all the meatballs in the pan, add cooked bell pepper mixture in it along with eggplant, stir in water and simmer for 30 minutes at low heat setting until thoroughly cooked.
6. Serve straight away.

## Nutrition:

Calories: 265 kcal Total Fat: 18 g Saturated Fat: 0 g Cholesterol: 47 mg Sodium: 153 mg Total Carbs: 12 g Fiber: 4.6 g Sugar: 0 g Protein: 17 g

## 202. SLOW-COOKED LEMON CHICKEN
by Elizabeth Gulley – Youngtown

**Preparation Time:** 20 minutes
**Cooking Time:** 7 hours
**Servings:** 4

### Ingredients:

- 1 teaspoon dried oregano
- ¼ teaspoon ground black pepper
- 2 tablespoons oil, unsalted

- 1-pound chicken breast, boneless, skinless
- ¼ cup chicken broth, low sodium
- ¼ cup water
- 1 tablespoon lemon juice
- 2 cloves garlic, minced
- 1 teaspoon fresh basil, chopped

## Directions:

1. Combine oregano and ground black pepper in a small bowl. Rub mixture on the chicken.
2. Melt the oil in a medium-sized skillet over medium heat. Brown the chicken in the melted oil and then transfer the chicken to the slow cooker.
3. Place chicken broth, water, lemon juice and garlic in the skillet. Bring it to a boil so it loosens the browned bits from the skillet. Pour over the chicken.
4. Cover, set slow cooker on high for 2½ hours or low for 5 hours.
5. Add basil and baste chicken. Cover, cook on high for an additional 15–30 minutes or until chicken is tender.

## Nutrition:

Calories: 197 kcal Total Fat: 9 g Saturated Fat: 5 g Cholesterol: 99 mg Sodium: 57 mg Total Carbs: 1 g Fiber: 0.3 g Sugar: 0 g Protein: 26 g

## 203. SMOTHERED PORK CHOPS AND SAUTÉED GREENS
by Merri Hall – New Rochelle

**Preparation Time:** 20 minutes
**Cooking Time:** 60 minutes
**Servings:** 6

### Ingredients:
### Smothered Pork Chops:

- 6 pork loin chops ("natural" center cut, bone-in)
- 1 tablespoon black pepper
- 2 teaspoons paprika
- 2 teaspoons granulated onion powder
- 2 teaspoons granulated garlic powder
- 1 cup and 2 tablespoons flour
- ½ cup canola oil
- 2 cups low-sodium beef stock
- 1½ cups fresh onions, sliced

- ½ cup fresh scallions, sliced on the bias

## Saute'ed Greens:

- 8 cups fresh collard greens, chopped and blanched
- 2 tablespoons olive oil
- 1 tablespoon oil
- ¼ cup onions, finely diced
- 1 tablespoon fresh garlic, chopped
- 1 teaspoon crushed red pepper flakes
- 1 teaspoon black pepper
- 1 teaspoon vinegar (optional)

## Directions:

1. Preheat oven to 350° F.

## Pork Chops:

1. Mix black pepper, paprika, onion powder and garlic powder together. Use half of mixture to season both sides of the pork chops and mix the other half with 1 cup flour.
2. Reserve 2 tablespoons of flour mix for later.
3. Lightly coat pork chops with seasoned flour.
4. Heat oil in large Dutch oven or oven-ready sauté pan (no rubber handles) on medium-high.
5. Fry pork chops for 2–4 minutes on each side or until desired crispness. Remove from pan and pour off all but 2 tablespoons of oil.
6. Cook onions until translucent, about 4–6 minutes. Stir in 2 tablespoons of reserved flour and mix well with onions for about 1 minute.
7. Slowly, add beef stock and stir until thickened.
8. Return pork chops to pan and coat with sauce. Cover or wrap with foil and cook in oven for at least 30–45 minutes at 350° F.
9. Remove from oven and let rest at least 5–10 minutes before serving.

## Saute'ed Greens:

1. To blanch greens, add greens to a pot of boiling water for 30 seconds.
2. Strain boiling water off and quickly transfer to ready bowl of ice and water.
3. Let cool, then strain and dry greens and set aside.
4. In large sauté pan on medium-high heat, meltoil and oil together. Add onions and garlic, cook until slightly browned, about 4–6 minutes.

5. Add collard greens and black and red pepper and cook for 5–8 minutes on high heat, stirring constantly.
6. Remove from heat; add vinegar if desired and stir.

### Nutrition:

Calories: 464 kcal Total Fat: 28 g Saturated Fat: 5 g Cholesterol: 71 mg Sodium: 108 mg Total Carbs: 26 g Fiber: 1.3 g Sugar: 0 g Protein: 27 g

## 204. AROMATIC HERBED RICE
### by Edward Mohn – Walnut Creek

**Preparation Time:** 10 minutes
**Cooking Time:** 15 minutes
**Servings:** 6

### Ingredients:

- 2 tablespoons olive oil
- 3 cups cooked rice (don't overcook)
- 4–5 cloves fresh garlic, sliced thin
- 2 tablespoons fresh cilantro, chopped
- 2 tablespoons fresh oregano, chopped
- 2 tablespoons fresh chives, chopped
- ½ teaspoon red pepper flakes
- 1 teaspoon red wine vinegar

### Directions:

1. In a large sauté pan, heat olive oil on medium-high heat and lightly sauté garlic. Add rice, herbs and red pepper flakes and continue to cook for 2–4 minutes or until well-mixed.
2. Turn off heat, add vinegar, mix well and serve.

### Nutrition:

Calories: 134 kcal Total Fat: 5 g Saturated Fat: 1 g Cholesterol: 0 mg Sodium: 6 mg Total Carbs: 21 g Fiber: 1.8 g Sugar: 0 g Protein: 2 g

# CHAPTER 17
# 3 - WEEKS MEAL PLAN

| 21 DAYS | BREAKFAST | LUNCH | DINNER |
|---------|-----------|-------|--------|
| WEEK 1 | | | |
| Day 1 | Vegetable Omelet | Baked Herbed Chicken | Mixed Pepper Paella |
| Day 2 | Mexican Style Burritos | Chicken and Cabbage Stir-Fry | Cauliflower Rice & Runny Eggs |
| Day 3 | Sweet Pancakes | Chicken and Leek Salad | Minted Zucchini Noodles |
| Day 4 | Breakfast Smoothie | Chicken Cranberry Sauce Salad | Lentil Vegan Soup |
| Day 5 | Buckwheat and Grapefruit Porridge | Curried Chicken Stir-Fry | Chickpea and Avocado Salad |
| Day 6 | Egg and veggie muffins | Thai-Style Chicken Salad | Vegetable and Tofu Skewers |
| Day 7 | Cherry berry bulgur bowl | Creamy Chicken | Vegan Alfredo Fettuccine Pasta |
| WEEK 2 | | | |
| Day 8 | Sausage Breakfast Casserole | Green Bean Veggie Stew | Saucy Fish Dill |
| Day 9 | French Toast with Applesauce | Cabbage Turkey Soup | Herbed Vegetable Trout |
| Day 10 | Bagels Made Healthy | Chicken Fajita Soup | Citrus Glazed Salmon |
| Day 11 | Cornbread with Southern Twist | Cream of Chicken Soup | Broiled Salmon Fillets |
| Day 12 | Grandma's Pancake Special | Turkey & Lemon-Grass Soup | Broiled Shrimp |
| Day 13 | Very Berry Smoothie | Beef Stroganoff Soup | Grilled Lemony Cod |
| Day 14 | Pasta with Indian Lentils | Green chicken enchilada soup | Spiced Honey Salmon |
| WEEK 3 | | | |
| Day 15 | Mexican Scrambled Eggs in Tortilla | Tuna Casserole | Roasted Chicken with Veggies & Mango |
| Day 16 | Raspberry Overnight Porridge | Fish Chili with Lentils | Roasted Chicken Breast |
| Day 17 | American Blueberry Pancakes | Sardine Fish Cakes | Grilled Chicken |
| Day 18 | Raspberry Peach Breakfast Smoothie | 4-Ingredients Salmon Fillet | Ground Chicken with Basil |
| Day 19 | Fast Microwave Egg Scramble | Spanish Cod in Sauce | Chicken &Veggie Casserole |
| Day 20 | Mango Lassi Smoothie | Salmon Baked in Foil with Fresh Thyme | Chicken & Cauliflower Rice Casserole |
| Day 21 | Breakfast Maple Sausage | Poached Halibut in Mango Sauce | Chicken Meatloaf with Veggies |

# CONVERSION TABLE

## VOLUME EQUIVALENTS (LIQUID)

| US STANDARD | US STANDARD (OUNCES) | METRIC |
|---|---|---|
| 2 tablespoons | 1 fl. oz. | 30 mL |
| ¼ cup | 2 fl. oz. | 60 mL |
| ½ cup | 4 fl. oz. | 120 mL |
| 1 cup | 8 fl. oz. | 240mL |
| 1½ cups | 12 fl. oz. | 355 mL |
| 2 cups or 1 pint | 16 fl. oz. | 475 mL |
| 4 cups or 1 quart | 32 fl. oz. | 1 L |
| 1 gallon | 128 fl. oz. | 4 L |

## OVEN TEMPERATURES

| FAHRENHEIT (°F) | CELSIUS (°C) APPROXIMATE |
|---|---|
| 250 °F | 120 °C |
| 300 °F | 150 °C |
| 325 °F | 165 °C |
| 350 °F | 180 °C |
| 375 °F | 190 °C |
| 400 °F | 200 °C |
| 425 °F | 220 °C |
| 450 °F | 230 °C |

## VOLUME EQUIVALENTS (LIQUID)

| US STANDARD | METRIC (APPROXIMATE) |
|---|---|
| 1/8 teaspoon | 0.5 mL |
| ¼ teaspoon | 1 mL |
| ½ teaspoon | 2 mL |
| 2/3 teaspoon | 4 mL |
| 1 teaspoon | 5 mL |
| 1 tablespoon | 15 mL |
| ¼ cup | 59 mL |
| 1/3 cup | 79 mL |
| ½ cup | 118 mL |
| 2/3 cup | 156 mL |
| ¾ cup | 177 mL |
| 1 cup | 235 mL |
| 2 cups or 1 pint | 475 mL |
| 3 cups | 700 mL |
| 4 cups or 1 quart | 1 L |
| ½ gallon | 2 L |
| 1 gallon | 4 L |

## WEIGHT EQUIVALENTS

| US STANDARD | METRIC (APPROXIMATE) |
|---|---|
| ½ ounce | 15 g |
| 1 ounce | 30 g |
| 2 ounces | 60 g |
| 4 ounces | 115 g |
| 8 ounces | 225 g |
| 12 ounces | 340 g |
| 16 ounces or 1 pound | 455 g |

# CONCLUSION

**M**anaging chronic kidney disease (CKD) requires lifestyle adjustments, but it might help to know that you're not alone. Over 31 million people in the United States are diagnosed with malfunctions of their kidneys or are battling kidney disease. As a registered dietitian (RD) with extensive experience assisting patients in taking control of their kidney disease, I have helped patients manage the physical symptoms associated with this disease and cope with the emotional toll that this life change can take. Without knowing what the future holds, uncertainty, fear, depression, and anxiety can be common. It may even feel like dialysis is inevitable, and you may be asking yourself if it is worth the time or effort to try and manage this stage of the disease or if it's even possible to delay the progression. As an expert in this field, I can assure you it is not just possible. It's yours to achieve—only 1 in 50 diagnosed with CKD end up on dialysis. So together, with the right tools, we can work to delay and ultimately prevent end-stage renal disease and dialysis. Success is earned through diet modifications and lifestyle changes. Using simple, manageable strategies, I have watched firsthand as my patients empowered themselves with knowledge. They have gone on to lead full, productive, and happy lives, continuing to work, play, and enjoy spending time with their loved ones—just the way it should be!

Only 1 in 50 diagnosed with CKD end up on dialysis

Diet is a vital part of CKD treatment, and it can help immensely in slowing the progression of the disease. Some Ingredients help the kidneys function, while others make the kidneys work harder. This has focused on crowding out the unhealthy with healthy and helpful. Also, targeting factors like salt and carbohydrate intake are important to reduce the risk of hypertension, diabetes, and other diseases resulting from kidney failure. I can't emphasize enough the importance of consulting a dietitian throughout CKD progression to optimize health. This is a good start, as it's designed specifically for the treatment of this population.

In this time of change and uncertainty, the knowledge you gain from these pages will give you the power to take your life into your hands and make changes to benefit you in the short and long term. I hope to educate and inspire you with new, easy ways to change your health trajectory. Adopting a kidney-friendly lifestyle can be challenging at first, but following these recipes will reduce the anxiety associated with selecting smart food options for your everyday life. And lest you worry that your new diet is restrictive or unsustainable, I want to assure you that these recipes are both easy and delicious, and they will give you a realistic, satisfying way to make this lifestyle change. This will guide you at each step of the way. Doing so will help take the stress of meal planning out of the equation and help you focus on the truly important things in life.

If your attempt at trying to prepare one of these recipes was particularly successful, why don't you share its picture on Amazon's Customer Review section? It might be helpful to those who, just like you, are looking for mouth-watering recipes, but without having to give up on a healthy lifestyle!

# PERSONAL NOTES

# PERSONAL NOTES

# PERSONAL NOTES

# PERSONAL NOTES

# PERSONAL NOTES

# PERSONAL NOTES

# PERSONAL NOTES

# PERSONAL NOTES

# PERSONAL NOTES

Printed in Great Britain
by Amazon

34669806R00077